He
Wins,
She
Wins

## Other books by Willard F. Harley, Jr.

*His Needs, Her Needs*
*Love Busters*
*Five Steps to Romantic Love*
*Draw Close*
*Fall in Love, Stay in Love*
*Buyers, Renters, and Freeloaders*
*Effective Marriage Counseling*
*His Needs, Her Needs for Parents*
*Defending Traditional Marriage*
*I Promise You*
*I Cherish You*
*Your Love and Marriage*
*Marriage Insurance*
*Give and Take*

# He
# WINS,
# She
# WINS

Learning the Art of Marital Negotiation

## Willard F. Harley, Jr.

Revell

*a division of Baker Publishing Group*
Grand Rapids, Michigan

© 2013 by Willard F. Harley, Jr.

Published by Revell
a division of Baker Publishing Group
P.O. Box 6287, Grand Rapids, MI 49516-6287
www.revellbooks.com

Printed in the United States of America

Library of Congress Cataloging-in-Publication Data
Harley, Willard F.
    He wins, she wins : learning the art of marital negotiation / Willard F. Harley, Jr.
      pages  cm.
      ISBN 978-0-8007-2251-7 (cloth)
      1. Marriage—Religious aspects—Christianity. 2. Conflict management—Religious aspects—Christianity. I. Title.
    BV835.H366 2013
    248.8′44—dc23                               2013016470

13  14  15  16  17  18  19       8  7  6  5  4  3  2

# Contents

# Introduction

Conflicts between spouses are inevitable. My wife, Joyce, and I face at least one every hour we're together. Our perspectives on how a problem should be solved are often entirely different. But in spite of those differences, we've become experts at resolving conflicts almost as soon as they arrive. And the skills we've developed in handling disagreements quickly and effectively have helped make our marriage everything we'd hoped it would be.

But what if we didn't know how to do that? What if our conflicts remained unresolved? What if we fought with each other or stonewalled each other instead of finding solutions? Conflicts would then pile up over the years. And by now, after fifty years of marriage, we would be drowning in unresolved conflicts. We wouldn't be able to tolerate living with each other.

When I was young, it was the norm for couples to marry, have kids, and raise those children together. Today, by contrast, the majority of adults are single, over 40 percent of children are raised by a never-married parent, and the percentage of adults choosing to marry is still dropping steadily. Those who do marry face the very real possibility of divorcing at some point.

In this book, I will focus attention on *one* of the reasons for this sea change in our culture—failure to negotiate successfully. When faced with conflicts, most couples do not know how to resolve them to their mutual satisfaction.

This is nothing new, of course. Marital therapists have been aware of this problem since the rate of divorce took off in the 1960s, and many books have been written to help couples communicate, understand, listen, and respect each other more effectively. So what can I offer that has not already been said?

What's different about my approach to resolving marital conflict is its ultimate goal: for a couple to be in love with each other. While most therapists view the resolution of martial conflict to be an end in itself, I view it as a means to an end. If a resolution builds your feeling of love for each other, I approve of it—it's been done the right way. If it fails to build that love, however, I believe you've made a mistake.

Throughout my counseling career, I've seen many couples who have no difficulty communicating with respect yet want to divorce because they have lost their love for each other. But I've never witnessed a couple who is in love *and* wants to divorce.

By reading this book, and applying its lessons to the way you handle conflicts, you will learn how to communicate effectively and resolve your conflicts—guaranteed. But you will learn something else that is far more important. You will learn how to do it in a way that will sustain your love for each other.

# PART 1

# The Art of Marital Negotiation

In the first section of this book, I'll focus on giving you the skills you need to become an artful negotiator. It won't be easy at first, but with time and practice you'll find that artful negotiation becomes a way of life for you and your spouse.

# 1

## Identifying the Problem

It had been a rough night. Little Emily, the newest addition to the Kramer family, didn't feel like sleeping. She felt like screaming. Her father, Tony, had buyers from China to entertain the next day at work, and he had to be at the top of his game. So each time Emily started crying, Tony would roll over and cover his head to block out the noise, figuring that his wife, Jodi, would get up to calm their distraught child.

Jodi, however, was quickly growing tired of being the one to get up to tend to the baby. She thought that she and Tony should take turns calming Emily down. After all, she was his daughter, too. And Jodi also needed her sleep—she had a busy day ahead of her as well.

So the third time Emily started to wail, Jodi decided it was Tony's turn to quiet her, and she tried to wake him up by poking him. When that didn't work she pushed him with her feet until finally he fell out of bed. When Tony cleared his head and realized what had happened to him, he flew into a rage.

"What's wrong with you?" he yelled.

"I'm sorry," Jodi explained. "But I couldn't wake you up and it's your turn to take care of Emily!"

Jodi and Tony understood their conflict over Emily's nighttime care. And they each had solutions to the problem that they felt were fair. Jodi proposed an equal division of responsibility—Tony would take care of the baby one time, and she would take care of her the next. Jodi would even have agreed to the two of them taking alternating days of the week—or even weeks of the month—just so the care would be equal.

Tony, however, felt that his alertness at work was too important to allow him to be wakened at night. Since he felt that Jodi's job did not require the same degree of vigilance that his did, he decided that she should be the only one to have her sleep interrupted.

This wasn't the first time Jodi and Tony had struggled with the issue of who would get up with the baby at night. In fact, the same problem had come up shortly after their first child, Robbie, was born. But they never resolved that difference of opinion and here they were again, another child later, still arguing about the same issue.

---

As I acknowledged in the introduction, conflicts between spouses are inevitable. Joyce and I face numerous conflicts in our marriage every day. We've learned how to resolve those conflicts the right way, and our marriage is strong as a result.

But what if, like Jodi and Tony, we found ourselves stuck in a pattern of conflict and were unable to resolve our issues? It wouldn't be long before we couldn't stand to be around each other.

## A Shift toward Equality

Historically, a husband has had the decisive edge when it came to resolving marital conflict. He simply made the decision and his wife dutifully submitted to it. In the past, most cultures and religions encouraged this. Husbands were to lead and wives were to follow. Marriage was often seen as a microcosm of the religious and political order where authority started at the top (God) and worked its way down. Men of greater rank had authority over men of lesser rank, and within a family, a husband had authority over his wife, children, servants, and slaves. Men dominated the world.

But in the United States the American Revolution began to turn that tradition on its head. The Declaration of Independence stated that everyone had an equal right to "life, liberty, and the pursuit of happiness." In practice, of course, those rights were not given to everyone overnight. It took almost a hundred years, but eventually slaves were freed, given citizenship, and African American males received the right to vote. Then, over fifty years later, women were finally included when they were given the right to vote and hold public office.

Today, in America and in most other democratic cultures, it's assumed that women should have the same basic rights as men. In marriage, that transformation has come to mean that women are to be equal partners with their husbands. It's no longer assumed that a husband has the right to dominate and control his wife.

Unfortunately, it's also no longer assumed that marriages will last a lifetime for couples. Prior to the 1960s, divorce rates were no higher than 10 percent, yet by 1980 they had soared to over 50 percent. Today, they have settled in at about 45 percent, but the percentage of couples marrying each year has been steadily dropping.

So what's the problem? Shouldn't marriages be happier today with both spouses working together rather than one being controlled by the other? It would seem so on the surface. But the trick, of course, is that men and women don't always see life the same way, and a cultural shift toward equality didn't magically equip them with the skills they need to face problems and make decisions jointly.

In many ways, marital decision-making would be less complicated for Joyce and me if we had lived a hundred years ago. Whenever we would have had a conflict, she would have been expected to submit to my way of doing things. As a caring husband, I might have listened to her point of view. But in the end, I would have made the final decision, which she would have had to accept.

When Joyce and I were married, it was still common to hear wives promising to "love, honor, and obey until death do us part," and Joyce dutifully recited that vow. Of course, like most men at that time, I didn't make the same commitment. I merely promised to "love and cherish" her.

But in spite of that wording in our vows, we both understood that we would be equal partners, gaining from each other's wisdom. Joyce would not simply *obey* me and I would not expect it of her. Instead, we would both love and cherish each other. And that meant making decisions jointly so that we would both be happy with them.

We didn't realize it at the time, but our decision to make our marriage a joint effort, with neither spouse having control over the other, was a radical departure from the way most marriages had functioned for thousands of years. And making joint decisions wasn't easy. It was far more difficult than it would have been if Joyce had simply obeyed me.

My experience as a marriage counselor has taught me that in today's marriages, negotiation is an essential skill for couples but one that is very difficult to learn. That's not to say that spouses don't know how to negotiate. In fact, many of the husbands and wives I've counseled are expert negotiators—outside of their marriage. But when it comes to negotiating with their spouses, they seem to ignore everything they know about the art of coming to an agreement.

This disconnect between our knowledge of negotiating and the way we actually negotiate in marriage probably has something to do with attitudes and instincts that have formed throughout human history with husbands dominating wives. Even though we live in a culture that gives women equal rights with men, many husbands still tend to approach conflicts as if their wives are still expected to "obey." And many wives, realizing the power that equality brings, use it to try to control their husbands.

When a conflict is not easily resolved, all too often a husband and wife both try to force each other to do what they want. And when that doesn't work, they try to go it alone, making unilateral decisions. The problem, of course, is that spouses don't want to be told what to do, and they also don't want their mate to make decisions that ignore their feelings and interests. Neither "short-cut" to conflict resolution solves the problem. And as with Tony and Jodi's childcare issues, these unresolved conflicts pile up, eventually overwhelming a couple with hopelessness.

Without a doubt, it's more complicated when a husband and wife make joint decisions rather than telling each other what to do or making unilateral decisions. But if a husband and wife are truly equal and want to resolve their conflicts once and for all, joint agreement is their only reasonable choice.

## A Common Goal

The place to start in any negotiation is to agree on the goal. And the goal I encourage couples to use when negotiating is to find a resolution that makes both of them happy—to find a win-win outcome. But as I mentioned earlier, it isn't easy to do. While most spouses would agree with me that win-win outcomes are the most desirable in marriage, many would argue that they're almost impossible to find. So, they would say, if a couple is to move on in life and make necessary decisions to keep functioning, compromise is inevitable. And by "compromise," they usually mean that the decisions should be somewhat less than win-win.

Charlie Weaver, former Minnesota governor Tim Pawlenty's chief of staff, has been a highly respected political negotiator. Throughout his boss's term as governor, he did a very admirable job of keeping highly contentious political foes in line by using his negotiating skill. He attributes his success to this goal: "Each party has to come away a little bit happy and a little bit mad."*

That goal might work for Mr. Weaver in politics, but it doesn't work very well in marriage. Spouses who try to resolve their conflicts with that goal in mind find that they almost immediately forget about the fact that the resolution made them "a little bit happy" and tend to remember forever how it made them "a little bit mad." Long-term resentment is a problem that almost every married couple experiences when conflicts are not resolved the right way—with both spouses happy with the outcome.

In politics, we can't expect everyone to be happy with a decision. There are just too many conflicting interests to accommodate. Besides, opposing parties have never promised to care for each other. Their goal is to defeat each other. But in marriage, only two people's interest must be taken into account when making a decision. And those two people should not be in competition with each other. In fact, they have made a unique and comprehensive commitment to care for each other. So it would make sense for them to strive for win-win outcomes whenever they face a conflict. And it's been my experience in my own marriage, and in

*Baird Helgeson, "Outline of budget deal at Capitol?" *Star Tribune*, April 23, 2011, http://www.startribune.com/printarticle/?id=120546354.

helping thousands of couples with their marriages, that this can be achieved by almost any couple.

I've written this book to help you get what you need from each other by becoming skilled marital negotiators. By the time you have finished reading it, and have applied what you've learned to the conflicts you face, you will be amazed at how successful you will have become at eliminating the conflicts that you may have been facing for years. And in the process of resolving all of your conflicts the right way, with win-win solutions, you will also find yourselves with something else—you'll be in love.

# 2

# Men and Women Need Each Other

Back in the days when I was a college professor, I taught neuropsychology. My students learned how the various parts of the brain control human behavior. I would begin the course by holding up an adult male brain and an adult female brain and ask the class if they noticed any differences. There was always overwhelming agreement that the brains didn't look at all the same. The male brain was bigger and lumpier than the female brain.

Then, as I dissected the two brains, I would show the class that they were not only different on the surface, but they were also different inside. The corpus callosum, a band of fibers that connects the two hemispheres, is much larger in the female brain, even though the brain itself is smaller. This greater interconnection between hemispheres may explain why women tend to take more information into account when making decisions than men do.

The inferior-parietal lobule is proportionately larger in the male brain, especially on the left hemisphere. This area of the brain was found to be abnormally large in Albert Einstein's brain and is associated with mathematical ability. Is this why more men than women tend to excel in mathematics?

Two language-associated structures, the superior temporal gyrus and the inferior frontal gyrus, are proportionately larger in the female brain. Is there any question that women tend to communicate more effectively than men?

The parietal region of the brain is thicker in the female brain. It's been suggested that such thickness inhibits a woman's ability to mentally rotate objects, thus giving men an advantage in understanding spatial relationships.

Beyond this host of visually identifiable differences, there are even more biochemical differences. For example, consider the contrasting ways in which estrogen in a female brain and testosterone in a male brain affect the hormone oxytocin, which has a calming influence and is released during stress. Estrogen enhances oxytocin's effect while testosterone reduces its effect. It's been suggested that this difference causes women to take care of themselves and their children under stress while men tend to have a fight or flight response.

How all these differences in the brains of men and woman actually affect behavior is still controversial. But the fact that there are important differences is clear. The overall physical differences that we all see in female and male bodies are also found in their brains—and in the way they think.

Years of counseling experience has led me to believe that those differences help men and women make the wisest decisions in life when they respect those differences. When those differences are not respected, they create conflict and turmoil.

## Men and Women Need Each Other's Perspective

The differences in the structure and internal chemistry of human male and female brains affect the way they think. So it should be no surprise to anyone that men and women come to different conclusions about a wide variety of issues.

Throughout recorded history, because men are physically stronger than women and therefore have been able to dominate them, a man's perspective has been regarded as correct (by men) and a woman's perspective as inferior. Until recently, even most women have accepted that interpretation of their judgment.

Just think about it for a moment. Why were women not allowed to vote or hold public office here in America until 1920? It's because the men who were in charge didn't think that women had sufficient wisdom. Their evidence was that women often didn't agree with their conclusions. And at the time, most women didn't seem to object to that characterization.

But that's no longer the case. We now know with certainty that women, on average, are just as smart as men. The two simply have somewhat different perspectives. In marriage, those differing perspectives often lead to conflict. And if a couple doesn't know how to come to an agreement with each other without one running over the other, conflicts lead to fights rather than to resolution. The result has been that spouses in most marriages grow apart, lose their romantic love for each other, and either live independently of each other or divorce.

It doesn't have to turn out that way, though. Husbands and wives can resolve conflicts the right way—with enthusiastic agreement. And the solutions they find as a result are far wiser than those originally considered by either spouse alone. Their differences in perspective complement each other to create a more complete understanding of the problems we all face in life. In other words, their joint agreement is the best resolution to their conflicts.

But there is an important caveat—they must hold each other's perspective in the highest regard. They must each assume that they don't have all of the answers and that their individual perspective may be somewhat flawed. They must value each other's point of view as an essential piece of the puzzle. They must understand that mutual enthusiastic agreement is the only goal to conflict resolution that makes sense in marriage.

It's the differences in the way men and women think that make them perfect partners in life. They need each other's brains. The biggest mistake a couple can make is to view their differing perspectives with contempt and condescension. To joke about the way men and women view life differently is to ignore their most valuable asset—their differences. And it's equally important for a couple to avoid the temptation to ignore their own perspective for the sake of the other.

## Why Giving In Isn't the Best Way to Care for Each Other

Most men and women know that they need each other in a host of ways: physically, emotionally, and intellectually. That dependence helps create an instinctive willingness to care for and protect each other that goes far beyond the way they treat same-sex relationships.

After speaking to a group of young mothers recently, I was asked this question: *My husband frequently "gives in" and lets me have my way, but I know that he's not really on board with it. I like when I get my way, but don't always feel good about it afterward. How do I get him to open up to me more about how he really feels?*

This woman's husband may have agreed to do what made her happy because he cared about her and wanted her to be happy.

She probably does the same for him every once in a while. They both had an instinct to care for each other at all costs, even if the cost is their own happiness.

But she was aware of a problem that this mutual care created for them. She liked to have her way, but deep down she knew that was not how they should be resolving conflicts.

Notice how she expressed her concern: she wanted him to "open up" so she could "know more about how he really feels." In other words, their discussions never really got down to their differences in perspective. Instead, she'd express what she wanted and he'd either deny her request or go along with it. What she really wanted, though, was a meeting of the minds—two entirely different minds.

When a choice is to be made in my marriage, my instinct often tells me, *If I really care about Joyce, I'll give her whatever she wants. And the more I'm willing to sacrifice my own pleasure for hers, the more caring I am.* And yet, I know that the wisest choices we can make are those that take both of our perspectives into account. They are equally valuable. So if I deny Joyce my perspective, I'm limiting our joint wisdom.

By simply giving his wife what she wanted without expressing his opinion, the husband of this young mother was depriving her of valuable information, and that made her feel very uncomfortable. It was more important to her to understand her husband than it was to get her way.

In marriage, a man and a woman should become a new entity, functioning not as two individuals but as a team. They should learn to plan together and to carry out that plan together. Having a cooperative and caring life partner gives us a great advantage over anything we could have been as an individual. And we're much wiser than we could have ever been on our own. But it takes skill to work as a team—negotiating skill.

# 3

## Why Win-Lose Doesn't Work

Before I show you how to find the best solutions to the problems you face in marriage (win-win outcomes), I will introduce some of the most common solutions where one spouse wins while the other loses. These win-lose outcomes are common because not only are they much easier to find than win-win outcomes but they are also somewhat instinctive. We seem to be naturally drawn to those kinds of solutions.

While dating and during the first few months of marriage, Tony and Jodi, our couple from the first chapter, could not have imagined having a fight over who would care for their child at night. During those years, they had expressed an eager willingness to help each other whenever a problem would arise, even if it meant sacrificing their own personal interests. If they had obtained premarital counseling, and the counselor had asked how they would be handling such a conflict, they would both have offered to care for the child so the other could rest. The conflict might have been seen as who would do the caring, with both of them offering their services.

## The Sacrifice Strategy

Sacrificing one's own interests for the interests of someone you love is a time-honored solution to many problems in life. It's regarded by many as being the ultimate form of care. The more spouses give sacrificially to each other, the more ideal their marriage is considered by some to be.

This ideal is described in the short story *The Gift of the Magi* by O. Henry. An impoverished couple wants to give each other something significant for Christmas but have no money to do so. The wife wants to give her husband a watch fob to go with his prized possession, his watch. The husband wants to give his wife a comb for her hair, her crowning glory. So he sells his watch to buy the comb and she sells her hair to buy the fob. It's a very sentimental story of sacrificial love, appropriate for the Christmas season when Christ was born to be the ultimate sacrifice for our sins.

But sacrifice has several pitfalls in marriage. First, sacrifice is usually done in secret. Instead of a couple working together on a solution to a problem, they work apart, keeping their plans to themselves. In the last chapter, I described the dilemma faced by a young mother. Her husband "gave in" and let her have her way. She liked getting her way, but she felt that in so doing, he was closing her out. She wanted him to open up so that she could know how he really felt. But personal sacrifice for the sake of someone you care for usually means that you don't reveal your innermost feelings. He can't give her what she wants and open up at the same time. Sacrifice usually prevents openness in marriage.

Second, sacrifice doesn't lead to long-term solutions to marital problems. At best, it's something that can be done only occasionally because the sacrificing spouse usually isn't willing to make it a habit. But it sets a precedent that leads to unsustainable expectations. When one spouse's gain is at the other spouse's voluntary loss, what was voluntary one day easily translates into an expectation that's demanded the next. For example, if on a special occasion a wife decides to sacrifice her own enjoyment, to have sex the way her husband wants to have it, sooner or later he'll be pestering her to do it the same way again until she gives in. Eventually, she will dread the very thought of sex because it's not done in a way that is enjoyable for her.

A third reason that sacrifice doesn't work well in marriage is that reciprocation is expected. If I do something that's unpleasant for me so that Joyce can have what she wants, I'll be waiting for her to return the favor. And if she doesn't do that—if I'm the only one making sacrifices—I'll assume that she doesn't care about me in the same way I care about her. Sooner or later my resentment will bubble to the surface.

In a mutually caring relationship such as marriage, sacrificing for each other doesn't make much sense if both spouses really do care about each other. Why should I expect Joyce to suffer for my happiness? Why should she expect me to suffer for her? Neither of us should want the other to lose so that we can gain. It's only if we are being selfish in an uncaring moment that we would expect the other to sacrifice. Mutual care means that both of us want each other to thrive and neither of us want the other to suffer.

So is there any place for sacrifice in marriage? I would suggest that it makes a great deal of sense to work together in *joint sacrifice* to accomplish a *goal of mutual value*. For example, my education was very difficult for both Joyce and me. We gave up many comforts and borrowed heavily to complete it. But my education was for our mutual advantage and eventually compensated for our joint sacrifice.

But joint sacrifice does not require secrecy. It's done in the open with both spouses knowing what will be involved, and what they will receive for their effort. It also has a well-defined ending—the sacrifice is not expected to last indefinitely. Finally, since the sacrifice is mutually agreed upon, requires joint effort, and benefits both spouses, there is no expectation of reciprocity.

So when I warn couples to avoid personal sacrifice, I want them to understand that, as tempting as it is for a mutually caring couple, it's a win-lose strategy. Don't do it if one gains at the expense of the other.

But if a couple can agree that a mutual short-term sacrifice for each of them can achieve a mutual long-term advantage for both of them, such a plan can actually be helpful to their marriage as long as basic emotional needs are met during the time of sacrifice.

## The Dictator Strategy

While the sacrifice strategy for resolving marital conflicts may seem on the surface to be the ultimate form of care, most other strategies with win-lose goals are not at all altruistic. Instead of "I'll lose so that you can win," they turn it around to be "You'll lose so that I can win." They're downright selfish. There should be no doubt that these strategies that lead to win-lose outcomes should be avoided. I'll begin my analysis with the traditional husband-in-charge approach that dominated society for millennia. I call it the **dictator strategy.**

---

### Are You a Dictator?

If you're not sure if you are a dictator, here are a few test questions. Do you ever tell your spouse what to do? Does a refusal trigger a disrespectful or even an angry reaction from you? Do you let your spouse know that there will be consequences for noncompliance? Do you require obedience from your spouse in some situations?

An even better test for dictatorship is to ask your spouse those questions about you. "Do I ever tell you what to do?" It's easy to see the dictator strategy in use when your spouse is the one using it. But when you use it yourself to try to get something accomplished, the fact that it's controlling and abusive is much more difficult to appreciate. *Someone must take charge or the job won't get done!* It's easy to justify.

---

For thousands of years it was customary for husbands to make all of the major decisions in marriage. A husband may have discussed the issue with his wife to gain her perspective, but that wasn't a given. And in the end his will usually prevailed.

But over the past few decades, this custom has changed, at least in most Western cultures. Consider for a moment the comedy program *Father Knows Best*. Can you imagine a show ever being given that name today? It originated on radio in 1949 with the father portrayed as lord of his kingdom. As the radio program morphed into television, the father's role softened, but he was still the boss right up through the last show in 1960.

By the time a similar comedy concept, *All in the Family*, appeared (1971–1983), comparison between the old and the new in marriage was the major premise. Archie Bunker's traditional dominant role contrasted with his modern son-in-law Michael's weak and confused role as husband. "Those Were the Days," the title of the show's theme song, made it clear that in Archie's view life sure was simpler when men ruled.

The changes in our culture that gave women the same rights as men were both long overdue and yet fraught with difficulty. For years, husbands had expected to be dictators. They would make the final decisions regarding the family, and their wives would dutifully obey them. In fact, obedience was a key promise in their wife's wedding vow.

But today you'll rarely hear the word "obey" mentioned in a woman's vows. Most often, today's wedding vows reflect equality for both spouses in marriage. Old habits, and traditions, do not die quickly, however. And to this day, many husbands keep trying to tell their wives what to do.

### Benevolent Dictators

When a husband uses the dictator strategy to resolve marital conflicts, he usually doesn't intend for it to hurt his wife and children. In fact, he'll typically argue that his decision is ultimately in the best interest of the entire family.

But even if a husband makes personal sacrifices as part of the process, most modern wives don't want their husbands to make unilateral decisions. They want to be equal partners in their lives together, and that includes decision-making. If a husband tries to force a decision upon his wife without consulting her, she finds it to be controlling and abusive. She doesn't want to live under the absolute authority of a husband.

Besides, what may seem benevolent to a husband may not be considered benevolent from a wife's perspective. If a final decision is not mutually agreeable to both spouses and instead is made unilaterally by the husband, it's very likely that the wife's interests are not being fully considered. I've witnessed many decisions made by husbands that were intended to be in the best interest of the family but turned into disasters. If the wife's reluctance to go forward would have put on the brakes, the family would not have suffered. A couple's decisions are usually much wiser when they both agree on a course of action.

Partnership is a key concept in modern marriages, and most women expect to make joint decisions with their husbands. Benevolent or not, a husband who expects to make all of the final decisions in marriage is often viewed as arrogant and disrespectful. After all, many women would argue, what right does a man have to make the final decisions? Isn't a woman's judgment just as wise—or sometimes even wiser?

### Wives Taking Charge

In the 1970s, women were encouraged to attend assertiveness training classes to resist the dictators in their lives. The gist of what they learned was to say "no" without having to explain why. At that time, many women still thought that they had to obey orders, especially the orders of their husbands. And a class teaching them how to say "no" was viewed as a first step in helping them gain control over their lives.

Today, most wives are beyond knowing how to say "no." In fact, many have now caught on to the traditional negotiating technique long employed by husbands—dictatorship. They've turned the tables by becoming the dictators themselves.

In decades past, a bossy wife would have been the butt of ridicule, with very uncomplimentary names ascribed to the woman who took charge in her family. But today, that's changed and the same woman may even be seen as a hero to some. No one bosses her around—she's the one who does the bossing.

Some husbands of such women have tried to accommodate their wife's leadership. Instead of challenging their wife's aggressive approach to problems, they try to simply fit in. When there is a conflict of opinion, these husbands capitulate to maintain peace. The adage "When mama ain't happy, ain't nobody happy" is taken to heart, and they do whatever they can to keep their wife happy, even at their own expense. Maybe that was what the husband was doing in my earlier example—when he "gave in" to his wife's wishes, he wasn't sacrificing, he was capitulating.

### Dueling Dictators

Some wives submit to the demands of their husbands, and some husbands do the same when their wives take charge. But a far more common response of husbands to dictator wives and wives to dictator husbands is to fight back. Arguments between dueling dictators are now so common in marriage that therapists have resorted to encouraging couples to "fight fair." Trying to resolve marital conflicts without fighting is often viewed not as a legitimate option but rather as wishful thinking.

Because you can usually see dictatorship for what it is when your spouse uses it but can't see it when you use it, the dueling dictator strategy becomes very common in marriages, especially after children arrive. Both Jodi and Tony were trying to force their will on the other when they fought over Emily's care, which made them both dictators. And it didn't work very well.

Can any spouse get away with a demand these days? Do you ever do what your spouse tells you to do? Even if you only occasionally oblige, I'll bet that you resent it. Yet I'll also bet that you make demands of your spouse—at least occasionally. You already know that it's a tactic that doesn't work very well with you, but you keep trying to make it work because you don't know what else to do.

The next time you make a demand of your spouse, imagine for a moment that he or she is using the same words and inflection to demand something of you. How would you react? You'd be more likely to fight than submit. That's what most spouses are doing when they try to resolve a conflict. They try to force their solutions on each other, and that usually leads to a duel.

## The Anarchy Strategy

A few years ago, as I was thumbing through an issue of *Reader's Digest*, I came upon an article entitled "The Science of a Happy Marriage," by Michael Gurian.* The subtitle of the article was particularly intriguing: "By nature, men and women aren't made for each other. How to outsmart our DNA and live happily ever after."

The thesis of this article was that couples experience five stages in marriage: (1) romance, (2) disillusionment, (3) power struggle, (4) awakening, and finally, (5) long-term marriage. We can all understand the romance, disillusionment, and power struggle stages, but what does he mean by awakening and long-term marriage? Awakening, Gurian explains, is coming to the awareness that romance is possible only in the beginning of a relationship and if a couple wants a long-term marriage they must give up hope for a romantic marriage. When that happens, the couple is able to settle into a long-term relationship.

In other words, in the best marriage each spouse goes his and her own way. Gurian claims that they should have different sets

*Michael Gurian, "The Science of a Happy Marriage," *Reader's Digest*, August 2004, 151–55.

of friends, create separate hobbies, go on separate vacations, and in general, create independent lifestyles. They experience a realization that they can remain married only if they have as little to do with each other as possible. After going through an irrational struggle to blend the lives of a man and a woman, something that's required in a romantic relationship, they finally realize that living independent lives is the only way for their marriage to survive.

Gurian, like many other spouses, likely experienced the results of the dueling dictators strategy for marital problem solving. That strategy does create a power struggle that seems endless and fruitless. What begins as a romantic relationship morphs into the worst nightmare a couple could have ever imagined. The caring lovers have become assassins.

So by his estimation, to remain married, a couple must give up on the illusion of ever maintaining a romantic relationship and rise to the realization that men and women are simply not meant to blend with each other for any length of time. They're just too different. Independent decision-making becomes the ultimate solution to marital conflicts.

Really? Is that what every couple must look forward to in life? Is that what you want your marriage to become?

You may have found, like Tony and Jodi, that the dueling dictators strategy doesn't resolve your marital conflicts, and in fact only makes matters worse. Maybe a man and a woman are so different that they can't be expected to blend their lives. So you may have started making at least some of your decisions independently of each other. If your spouse doesn't want to cooperate with you, then your only other hope for survival is to go it alone. I call this the **anarchy strategy** for resolving marital conflicts. And it's yet another win-lose strategy that doesn't work.

The good news is that, contrary to what Mr. Gurian and others may want you to believe, it's *not* your only option. Unfortunately most couples don't realize this before having to learn the hard way how win-lose strategies fail to solve their problems.

## The Anatomy of a Conflict

Let's return to my opening illustration of Tony and Jodi's marital conflict: Who should get up with little Emily at night?

When their first child, Robbie, had arrived, Tony had suggested that Jodi should get up to care for him at night because his job required greater mental alertness than her job. At first, she willingly sacrificed her own sleep so that Tony could be well rested. But as time went on, she felt that it was unfair to her.

By the time little Emily arrived, Jodi was no longer in agreement with the arrangement. She suggested that Tony take turns with her. But he refused and demanded that she take sole responsibility for Emily's care at night. He had become a dictator.

Jody tried to submit to his demands for a few days, but eventually decided to take matters into her own hands. So when Emily was crying, she pushed him out of bed to make her point. She had become a dueling dictator.

Of course, the dueling dictatorship strategy didn't solve the problem for them. Instead, it triggered a fight. Each had their own perspective of how the conflict should be resolved and tried to force it on the other. When his demand was not met, Tony told Jodi that she was not being a good wife and mother by refusing to get up each time Emily cried at night. Jodi in turn told Tony that he was being selfish in assuming that she should be the only parent caring for their children.

The name-calling escalated to such a point that they were both screaming obscenities at each other, which woke up Robbie. Now both of their children were crying and the parents couldn't even hear it over their own voices.

That fight became a turning point in their marriage, at least for Jodi. She came to the conclusion that arguing was pointless because it didn't solve anything. So she did what she thought would be the wisest alternative: make some decisions as if Tony didn't exist.

Regarding the conflict at hand, Jodi decided that she would take care of the children when they cried at night, not because Tony told her to do it but because he wouldn't do it and she wanted them to be comforted. However, the next time he wanted something from her, he would discover that he'd be on his own.

Jodi began using the anarchy strategy for resolving conflicts: she did whatever she pleased.

At first, Tony was happy that Jodi let him sleep at night. He knew that she was upset with him and had become emotionally distant, but he had important business to transact and didn't have time to think about Jodi's issues.

But as the days and weeks followed, Jodi's independence became increasingly upsetting to Tony. She lived her life without letting him know what she was doing or where she was going. Some evenings, after he arrived home, she would get in the car and drive off, returning after midnight. When he wanted to know where she was, she said it was none of his business.

Tony tried to fight with Jodi when she would just take off, but she wouldn't fight back. She had her own car, her own checking account, and her own cell phone. She wouldn't discuss any issue with him, including why she refused to make love. He eventually decided that, to avoid a divorce, he should adopt the same approach: he would do whatever he pleased. Now they were both using the anarchy strategy to solve their problems and were headed down a dangerous path.

So what should they have done instead? That's what we're about to find out.

# 4

## Keeping Romantic Love in Mind

So far, I've focused attention on one of the reasons that win-lose outcomes in marital negotiation are terribly flawed: in today's marriages they simply don't get the job done. They usually don't resolve the conflict. Whoever is on the losing end doesn't usually accept the result. They either fight to gain the upper hand at a later time or they go it alone, taking matters into their own hands. In either case, the problem persists.

While it's true that Jodi did get up with Emily after their fight, and continued to do so during the following weeks, the issue was not settled. The "solution" and the way it was decided caused her to feel deep resentment toward Tony every time she thought about it.

The bitter feeling that she harbored led to another reason that win-lose outcomes are terribly flawed: they destroy romantic love in marriage. I'll explain why that happens by introducing you to a metaphor that I've created to help couples understand why everything they do and every decision they make affects their love for each other. I call it the Love Bank.

## The Love Bank Never Closes

There is a Love Bank inside each one of us. Our emotions use it to keep track of the way people treat us. Every person we've ever known has an account in our Love Bank and their balances are determined by how we feel when we are with them. If someone makes us feel good, "love units" are deposited into their account. But if we feel bad around this person, love units are withdrawn. The better we feel the more love units are deposited. The worse we feel the more are withdrawn.

Our emotions use the balance in each person's Love Bank account to advise us as to whether or not that person should be a part of our life. And they do so by making that person attractive or repulsive to us. When someone has a positive Love Bank balance—more deposits than withdrawals—our emotions encourage us to spend time with that person by making us "like" him or her. But when someone has a negative balance—more withdrawals than deposits—our emotions encourage us to run for cover by causing us to "dislike" that person.

The larger the positive balance in someone's Love Bank account, the more attracted we are to that person. For example, if two hundred love units accumulate, we feel pretty good about someone; if five hundred love units accumulate, we may consider that person to be one of our best friends.

But something special happens when the Love Bank balance of someone of the opposite sex reaches a critical threshold of, say, one thousand love units. Our emotions give us an extra incentive to spend as much time as possible with that person—even for the rest of our lives. It's the feeling of incredible attraction that we call romantic love.

Of course, negative balances have the opposite effect. Just like a checking account, a Love Bank account can be in the red when love units continue to be withdrawn after none are left. If someone at work has a Love Bank balance of negative two hundred because of his annoying habits, our emotions will make us feel uncomfortable whenever he's around, even when he's not doing anything that's annoying. And someone with a Love Bank balance of negative five hundred will seem downright repulsive. Our emotions want us to avoid those who make us feel badly, and they do it by making that person seem unattractive to us.

But when someone has a very large negative balance, say, negative one thousand love units, our emotions go to very great lengths to encourage us to avoid *all* contact. That's when we end up "hating" that person. It happens automatically if someone's balance in our Love Bank dips to that critical low point.

We don't end up reaching that hate threshold with most people because we stop having contact with them long before their Love Bank balance falls that far. If you work with a very rude and inconsiderate person, you can request another office and simply avoid contact as much as possible. Even if it's your next-door neighbor, you can try to ignore that person, or even move if necessary. It's possible to escape from just about everyone who upsets you, thus putting an end to Love Bank withdrawals.

But in marriage, escape isn't so easy. Day after day, week after week, month after month, if you're forced to be with a spouse who keeps making Love Bank withdrawals, you eventually feel so repulsed that divorce seems to be the only way out. What once was the feeling of romantic love when Love Bank balances were overflowing has become the feeling of deep and persistent revulsion.

And it's all due to an extremely important reality in marriage: *just about everything that you and your spouse do affects the way you feel about each other. What you do either builds your love for each other or it destroys that love.*

One bad experience won't ruin a couple's love for each other, of course. But the way couples make decisions, and the decisions themselves, can certainly do the job if win-lose outcomes are the norm.

The argument about who should get up to quiet Emily down made massive Love Bank withdrawals from both Tony's and Jodi's accounts, and the decision itself made more withdrawals from Tony's account in Jodi's Love Bank every time it was implemented. But that conflict was not an isolated incident. The same thing happened when other conflicts were confronted. Just two days earlier, Tony had come home from work ahead of Jodi and started playing a video game. When she arrived after picking up the children from daycare, he continued playing the game, which upset Jodi.

"Why are you playing a video game when you know that the children are hungry? Why didn't you start dinner?" she shouted. "What kind of a father are you?"

Tony lashed back. "At least I came home on time. What were you doing that was so important?"

It's not that the issue of who-should-do-what after coming home from work hadn't been discussed before. Tony and Jodi had fought over that issue almost every week. But they had not come to an agreement. Tony wanted Jodi to be fully responsible for the children's meals, and Jodi wanted Tony to help her. But they had not reached an agreement. So Tony did what he thought was right: play video games to help him relax after a hard day's work.

Most women reading this illustration can understand Jodi's frustration with Tony. They may have experienced something very similar when their children were young. And they would agree with the main point I'm making in this chapter: failure to resolve conflicts to the satisfaction of both spouses can destroy the love spouses have for each other.

The decisions Tony made benefitted him at Jodi's expense. By associating him with the resentment those decisions caused, massive withdrawals were made from his account in her Love Bank. What once had been a feeling of incredible attraction turned into repulsion because they failed to find win-win outcomes to this and other common conflicts.

## Win-Lose Outcomes Had Been the Norm

During the time that they dated and even in the first few years of marriage, conflicts between Tony and Jodi had been very rare because their lives had been relatively simple. But when a conflict did arise, they tended to respond sacrificially. They did whatever it took to make each other happy, even when it wasn't in their own interest to do so. They had been eager to help each other without having to be asked because they were in love. They both tried to do what the other seemed to expect of them, and they avoided anything that might be disappointing. They went out of their way to demonstrate the care that they felt toward each other.

But after their first child arrived and their responsibilities grew exponentially, life had become more stressful for both of them. They depended more on each other to pick up the slack, but they had not learned how to ask each other for help. At some point between their first and second child, they both felt that their care was a one-way street. They both felt that they were giving far more than they were getting. So instead of giving sacrificially to each other, they started to take selfishly from each other.

We've already discussed some of the problems inherent in sacrificial giving: a lack of openness, an unsustainable precedent, an expectation of sacrifice in return, and an ever-increasing resentment when expectations are not fulfilled. But there's yet another problem. It can destroy romantic love.

You'd think that giving sacrificially in marriage would actually build romantic love. And it can seem that way if a couple's conflicts are few and simple, like they were when Tony and Jodi were dating. But when life gets complicated, especially after children arrive, it's more obvious that sacrifice is a failed strategy because it doesn't lead to win-win outcomes. And win-lose outcomes do not resolve a conflict.

As problems came crashing down on Tony and Jodi like ocean waves, unrelenting and daunting, they needed to know how to deal with them quickly and correctly. But because they had failed to learn those lessons, they were unprepared for the inevitable.

Those who feel that romantic love is fleeting in marriage and can be expected to survive only during the earliest years of the relationship should spend some time with couples who have experienced a lifetime of romantic love. What are these couples doing that makes their marriages so romantic? Is it their personalities? Have they found their perfect match and are unusually compatible? Do they have a high level of commitment to each other?

Or is it that they have learned how to resolve conflicts in a way that maintains their love with each other?

I call what Joyce and I have had for fifty years of marriage *extraordinary care*. We don't use the most common conflict-resolution strategies in marriage—those that pit one spouse against the other, leading to disillusionment and a power struggle. Instead, we find solutions that build partnership and trust. We search for win-win outcomes whenever we have a conflict.

This metaphor of the Love Bank can help you understand what it will take for you to be in love with each other throughout life: make as many deposits as possible and avoid making withdrawals. Keep your Love Bank balance well above one thousand. I wrote *His Needs, Her Needs* to help couples learn how to make very large Love Bank deposits by meeting each other's most basic emotional needs. And then I wrote *Love Busters* to help couples avoid common habits that lead to Love Bank withdrawals. I've also created two questionnaires—the Emotional Needs Questionnaire (appendix B) and the Love Busters Questionnaire (appendix C)—that will help you identify your most important emotional needs and the most damaging habits that may be eroding your love for each other. You may copy them in an enlarged format so you will have plenty of space to write your answers. They may also be downloaded free of charge from the questionnaires section of the Marriage Builders website (www.MarriageBuilders.com).

If your answers in the Emotional Needs Questionnaire indicate that you need help learning how to meet each other's most important emotional needs, read *His Needs, Her Needs*. And if your answers in the Love Busters Questionnaire indicate that you need help overcoming habits that are destroying your romantic love for each other, read *Love Busters*.

But in this book I focus on a third way for you to keep your Love Bank balances high: to make decisions that lead to win-win outcomes instead of win-lose outcomes. Win-win outcomes are the only way to make deposits into each other's Love Banks simultaneously.

# 5

## A Win-Win Strategy

Ed had a little extra time on his hands between appointments. His next real estate appraisal was in two hours, and he was completely caught up on his paperwork. So he decided to take the spare time to shop for a new refrigerator. The one in his apartment worked okay, but it was one that he'd inherited from his grandfather. It was a gas refrigerator that was over sixty years old.

As he walked into the appliance store, he was immediately greeted by a salesman who asked what he would like to see. When he mentioned refrigerators, the salesman cheerfully directed him to the rows upon rows of them, in all shapes and sizes. When the salesmen asked Ed how much space he had for it, Ed was startled to learn that there would be plenty of space because it would be replacing a big, clunky gas refrigerator.

After arriving at a model in the size that reflected his eating habits, Ed asked the salesman a crucial question: *What advantages would a new refrigerator have over my old one?*

The salesman responded by describing individual spaces in the refrigerator that would keep particular types of food freshest, the economic advantages, and its modern appearance. Then he made an offer that was hard to refuse: *We'll remove your old refrigerator, install the new one, and if in two weeks you don't agree that this was one of your best decisions of the year, we will take our refrigerator back and put your old refrigerator in its original place—at no charge at all to you.*

Ed agreed to the salesman's offer and became the proud owner of a new, modern refrigerator, and two weeks later he was happy that he'd made the purchase.

Business negotiators have learned to do something that still eludes politicians: they know how to negotiate with the interest of the opposing party in mind. In business, the opposing party is your customer—an essential ingredient of your success. So if, in the words of Charlie Weaver, your goal is to leave your customer "a little bit happy and a little bit mad," you wouldn't have much of a chance in business.

The goal of salespeople's negotiation with customers is to deliver a product that they are enthusiastically willing to buy at a price that is profitable for the company. It's a win-win goal, and it's achieved many times every second throughout the world. If the average business can do it, why can't the average marriage also do it?

## Why Do Couples Resist a Win-Win Goal?

A win-win outcome both in business and in marriage is the ideal. No one would argue that point. But as I've already noted, some feel that trying to achieve that ideal in marriage is immoral, impossible, or impractical. They feel that there's something about a romantic relationship between a man and a woman that rules out win-win resolutions to conflict.

The problem usually begins with confusion over the value of the sacrifice strategy—one partner is willing to lose so that the other partner can win. It's a time-honored way to prove that you care, and it's the way most romantic relationships begin. It gives your account in a prospective mate's Love Bank an initial boost.

It's a lot like the way a business introduces a new product. It's sold at a greatly reduced price, or is even given away, to give prospective customers a taste of what the business can do for them. In a dating relationship, partners want an opportunity to get to know each other, so they will often sacrifice their own interests to motivate each other to spend time together. When I would call Joyce for a date, she would agree to go even before I told her what we'd be doing.

But it's at this point that business and romantic relationships usually part. In business, the product that had been initially given away is now priced to provide a profit for the company and value for the customer. In romantic relationships, however, sacrifice continues to be expected. After all, it's regarded as the romantic ideal.

Fortunately for our marriage, after we said our vows Joyce stopped sacrificing her interests just to be with me. If we were to go on a date, she wanted to know where we'd be going before she'd agree to go. And if she wasn't interested in what I had in mind, she'd suggest alternatives that served her interests. The sacrifice strategy had come to an end in our marriage, as it does in all romantic relationships.

Why was this fortunate for our marriage? Because we were now forced to do what businesses do—find win-win outcomes to our conflicts.

Of course, we could have chosen the path that most romantic relationships follow: dictatorship, dueling dictators, and anarchy. In time, we would have become disillusioned, had a power struggle, lost our love for each other, and eventually parted ways either through divorce or permanent separation.

But we didn't follow that path, and as a result, we are still in a romantic relationship after fifty years of marriage. I'm convinced that every couple can follow the path we've taken by learning to resolve their conflicts with each other's interests in mind. When that happens, they discover win-win solutions to all of their conflicts.

## The Policy of Joint Agreement

To help couples keep their eye on the ball, I challenge them to consider a rule that leads to win-win outcomes. I call it the Policy of Joint Agreement: *Never do anything without an enthusiastic agreement between you and your spouse.* Enthusiastic agreement becomes the goal of negotiation whenever a couple faces a conflict. In other words, they both must win or they keep negotiating.

If you follow the Policy of Joint Agreement (POJA), it will force you to resolve conflicts the right way—the way that takes the interests of both of you into account simultaneously. Not only is this the mutually caring thing to do, but final decisions made this way are usually wiser than any decision you would have made on your own. By joining together to make each decision, you're able to consider a much broader range of options, and come to conclusions that take more factors into account.

When I first introduce this rule to clients, it usually triggers two reactions. At first people react to how they feel about being consulted before their spouse makes a decision: "If this means that Lisa must ask me how I feel about what she's planning to do before she does it, I think that's a good idea. There's a lot going on in her life that I'd like to know about, and a lot that I wouldn't agree with if I did know. If she'd tell me her plans in advance, and give me the right to veto some of them, I think we'd get along a lot better."

But it doesn't take long for a second reaction to unfold—how they feel about being required to have their spouse's agreement before *they* can do anything: "It would be ridiculous to let Lisa keep me from doing what I have to do. Sometimes she just doesn't understand, and so I have to make decisions she doesn't like.

---

### Why "Enthusiastic" Agreement?

In most marriages, a simple agreement can be challenging. So why do I insist on "enthusiastic" agreement? Doesn't that requirement make difficult decisions seem impossible?

Unless you have enthusiastic agreement, it's tempting to settle for reluctant agreement, where one spouse goes along with what the other wants just to get along. In that case, rather than winning, the reluctant spouse actually loses.

But reluctant agreement not only leaves one spouse on the short end of the deal, it can also lead to failure to follow through. Have you ever had an agreement with your spouse that was not fulfilled? Your spouse agreed to do something for you and then didn't do it. Usually such failure to follow through on an agreement is the result of a reluctant agreement. At the time of the agreement, your spouse felt pressured to agree, but when the time came to carry out the task, he or she lacked the motivation to do so. Such behavior is not only very frustrating but also makes agreements essentially meaningless.

Enthusiastic agreement solves that problem. When an agreement is clearly in the interest of both spouses, follow-through is rarely a problem. It's in both spouses' best interest to keep their commitments, and their agreements can be trusted.

---

I don't think her 'feelings' should keep me from achieving my personal goals."

This introduces the problem of empathy. We all want our spouse to be considerate of our feelings because we feel what our spouse does to us. But we tend to be inconsiderate of our spouse's feelings because we don't feel what we do to them. If we were emotionally connected to each other so that we would feel what each of us does to the other, we'd behave very differently. We'd want to know how our behavior would affect each other—in advance—so we would avoid any discomfort to ourselves.

Without such an emotional connection, the POJA is the next best thing. It forces us to give advance notice of how we will be affecting each other. While we can't actually feel our effect on each other, it makes us behave as if we did.

## "How Do You Feel?"

The Policy of Joint Agreement helps you to become sensitive to each other's feelings, especially when you don't feel like doing so. Since you're required to have each other's enthusiastic agreement before you do anything, it forces you to ask each other a very important question: *How do you feel about what I would like to do (or what I would like you to do for me)?*

That simple question and its answer helps you build a crucial understanding of each other. You may not actually feel what your spouse feels, but at least you give your spouse the opportunity to tell you how he or she feels. And then, even when you find yourself in a thoughtless mood, the POJA forces you to be thoughtful.

You are now a team, no longer two independent individuals. As life partners, you should work together to achieve objectives that benefit both of you simultaneously. Why should one of you consider your own interests to be so important that you can run roughshod over the interests of the other? That's a formula for marital disaster. A team can't survive if each member is pulling against the other.

When I first see a couple in marital crisis, they are usually living their lives as if the other hardly exists, making thoughtless decisions regularly because they don't care how the other feels. As a result, when I introduce the Policy of Joint Agreement, it seems totally irrational to them. Their way of life is based on so many inconsiderate habits that the policy seems to threaten their very existence.

At first, neither spouse wants to abandon their thoughtless and insensitive lifestyle. But I challenge them to try it for just a few weeks, and the more they try following the policy, the easier it becomes to reach agreement. They replace thoughtless decisions with those that take each other's feelings into account. And they develop real compatibility—building a way of life that is comfortable for both of them.

I think you can see why thoughtless behavior ruins a marriage. It not only creates massive Love Bank withdrawals, destroying romantic love, but it also proves that spouses don't really care about each other. If they did care, they would be thoughtful of each other—they would make decisions that take each other's feelings into account.

No wonder so many people are disillusioned by marriage. I'd be disillusioned too if Joyce were to ignore my feelings when she makes decisions. But that's not the way it has to be. It's certainly not the way it's been in our marriage. By making our decisions together, Joyce and I demonstrate our care for each other, and as a result, our marriage continues to be very fulfilling for both of us.

When a couple makes a commitment to share power and control with each other by following the POJA, their lives begin to blend and their love for each other grows. At that point they are using what I call the **democracy strategy** to resolve their conflicts.

## The Democracy Strategy—Effective, but Difficult to Use

The democracy strategy has none of the disadvantages of the other four strategies we've discussed—sacrifice, dictator, dueling dictators, or anarchy. Instead of failing to resolve conflicts, it succeeds. Instead of destroying romantic love, it builds it. It's the only reasonable way that a husband and wife should make decisions.

But as successful as democracy has been in world politics, it's difficult to implement and it's complicated. The same is true for democracy in marriage. It requires training, creativity, and patience.

In the next chapter, I'll describe the training you should have that will give you the skills you need to resolve marital conflicts the right way. If you follow this training program, you'll eventually find yourselves solving some of the most difficult problems you've ever faced in marriage. And those solutions will help make your marriage everything you'd hoped it would be.

# 6

## Negotiators, Take Your Places

I hope that by now you are convinced that win-win solutions to marital conflicts should be your goal. But you still may not quite be sure how to actually reach an enthusiastic agreement. After all, democracy isn't easy. And neither is marital negotiation using the democracy strategy. But for civilizations and marriages alike, the rewards found in considering the interests of others are well worth the added effort.

Unlike the sacrifice strategy, the dictator strategy, the dueling dictators strategy, and the anarchy strategy, the goal of the democracy strategy is *mutual thoughtfulness*. Those other strategies miss the very point of marriage. They don't lead to a blending of two lives the way the democracy strategy does. Instead they ultimately cause a couple to grow apart.

If you want to grow in compatibility and love for each other, the first step you must take is to accept the Policy of Joint Agreement as the rule you will live by for the rest of your lives together. That rule helps create the question, *How do you feel about what I'd like to do, or what I'd like you to do for me?*

When the question is asked and you receive a negative response, *I wouldn't be enthusiastic about it*, the POJA offers you two choices: either abandon the idea or try to discover alternative ways of making it possible—with your spouse's enthusiastic agreement. And that's where negotiation begins.

With practice, you and your spouse can become experts at getting what you need from each other. Once you agree to this policy, fair and effective negotiation will become a way of life for you. And you'll also be forced to abandon the strategies you may have been using that have led to arguments and the loss of love.

At first, asking the question "How do you feel about . . ." will seem very strange to you, and possibly even humorous. That's to be expected, because any new behavior usually seems awkward at first. Yet that question is at the very core of every fair negotiation in life, and you must force yourselves to ask it until it becomes a habit. Then it will feel natural to you.

But even after you've agreed to follow the Policy of Joint Agreement, you may not understand what goes on between the question and the enthusiastic agreement. You may not have had much experience negotiating effectively with each other.

So I suggest that you learn to follow a step-by-step procedure that is used by almost all successful negotiators. First I'll explain the basic guidelines and give you a chance to use them with simple conflicts that are not emotionally charged (such as grocery shopping). Then, when you have learned to follow the guidelines, we'll tackle the real conflicts that you have been facing.

## Four Guidelines for Successful Negotiation

### *Guideline #1: Set ground rules to make negotiation pleasant and safe.*

Most couples view discussion of a conflict as a walk through a minefield. That's because their efforts are usually fruitless and they come away from the experience battered and bruised. Who wants to try to negotiate when you have nothing but disappointment and pain to look forward to? So before you begin to negotiate, set some basic ground rules to make sure that you will both enjoy the discussion. Since you should negotiate as often as conflict arises, it should always be a pleasant and safe experience for you both.

To help you achieve that outcome, I suggest three basic ground rules.

GROUND RULE #1: TRY TO BE PLEASANT AND CHEERFUL THROUGHOUT YOUR DISCUSSION.

A conflict can create a negative emotional reaction so quickly that you may think you can't control it. But with practice, you can do what most negotiators learn to do—be cheerful in the face of adversity.

I realize that you will view the refrigerator salesman's situation to be completely different than yours. He can distance himself emotionally from a sale much more easily than you can with a marital conflict. But take my word for it: effective negotiation, whether in business or in marriage, requires a smile.

GROUND RULE #2: PUT SAFETY FIRST—DO NOT MAKE DEMANDS, SHOW DISRESPECT, OR BECOME ANGRY WHEN YOU NEGOTIATE.

Once the cat is out of the bag and you've told each other what you'd like to do, what you would like the other person to do, or what's bothering you, you've entered one of the most dangerous phases of negotiation. If your feelings have been hurt, you're tempted to retaliate. And unless you make a special effort to resist demands, disrespect, and anger, you will revert to the dueling dictators strategy and your negotiation will turn into an argument. But if you can keep each other safe from your own abusive instincts, your intelligence will help you find the solution you both need.

> GROUND RULE #3: IF YOU REACH AN IMPASSE WHERE YOU DO NOT SEEM TO BE GETTING ANYWHERE, OR IF ONE OF YOU IS STARTING TO MAKE DEMANDS, SHOW DISRESPECT, OR BECOME ANGRY, STOP NEGOTIATING AND COME BACK TO THE ISSUE LATER.

Just because you can't resolve a problem at a particular point in time doesn't mean you can't find an intelligent solution in the future. Don't let an impasse prevent you from giving yourselves a chance to think about the issue. Let it incubate for a while, and you'll be amazed what your minds can do.

If your negotiation turns sour and one of you succumbs to the temptation of becoming a dictator (demands, disrespect, or anger), end the discussion by changing the subject to something more pleasant. After a brief pause, the offending spouse may apologize and wish to return to the subject that was so upsetting. But don't go back into the field until it has been swept clear of mines.

### Guideline #2: Identify the conflict from both perspectives.

Once you've set ground rules that guarantee a safe and enjoyable discussion, you're ready to negotiate. But where do you begin? First, you must state the conflict and then try to understand it from the perspective of both you and your spouse.

Most couples go into marital negotiation without doing their homework. They don't fully understand the conflict itself, nor do they understand each other's perspective. In many cases, they aren't even sure what they really want.

So, at least while you are first learning to resolve your conflicts the right way, I recommend that each of you use a notebook (or smartphone) to document everything you learn about a certain conflict. On the first page, state the issue. What do you want to do, or want your spouse to do for you? Then, on the next few pages, describe each other's conflicting perspective. You might put a happy face at the top of each page to remind you to be cheerful. In the margin, remind yourself to avoid demands, disrespect, and anger. An example of how your notebook should be laid out can be found in appendix A, the Marital Negotiation Worksheet. Use it as a guide to help you find win-win solutions to any conflict you face.

Respect is key to success in negotiation, and it's particularly important in this information-gathering phase. Once the problem has been identified, and you hear each other's perspective, try to understand each other instead of trying to straighten each other out. Remember that your goal is enthusiastic agreement, and that can't happen if you reject each other's perspective out of hand. You may eventually be able to respectfully change each other's point of view, but that should be attempted only after you thoroughly understand it. The only way you'll reach an enthusiastic agreement is to find a solution that accommodates both of your perspectives.

This last point is so important that I will state it another way: *you will not solve your problem if you are disrespectful of each other's perspective. Both perspectives must be accommodated.* In this stage of negotiation, you are to simply gather information that will help you understand what it will take to make each other happy. If you reject the information provided by your spouse, you will be ignoring the facts. You should not interrupt or talk over each other, or even use mannerisms (such as rolling your eyes) that could be interpreted as disrespectful.

It's much easier to negotiate the right way when your goal is enthusiastic agreement. It helps eliminate all the strategies that attempt to wear each other down with abuse. But when some couples can't be demanding, disrespectful, or angry, they feel helpless about discussing an issue. They're so accustomed to being dictators that being respectful seems unnatural and phony. They feel as if they are communicating at a superficial level when they're actually learning how to communicate at a much greater depth of understanding.

Is that how you and your spouse feel? If so, remember that with practice you'll begin to feel more comfortable approaching every conflict with respect and the goal of mutual agreement. You'll learn to ask each other questions, not to embarrass each other or to prove each other wrong, but to gain a fuller understanding of what it would take to make each other happy. And when you think you have the information you need to consider win-win solutions, you're ready for the next step.

### Guideline #3: Brainstorm with abandon.

You've set the ground rules. You've identified the problem and discovered each other's perspective. Now you're ready for the creative part—looking for mutually acceptable solutions. I know that can seem impossible if you and your spouse have drifted into incompatibility. But the climb back to compatibility has to start somewhere, and if you put your minds to it, you'll think of options that please you both.

You will be tempted to sacrifice—to give in to your spouse's wishes. But as I have mentioned earlier, that approach will ultimately get you into trouble. It's not a win-win outcome. Your goal should be mutual happiness with neither of you gaining at the other's expense.

You also won't get very far if you allow yourself to think, *If she really loves me she'll let me do this*, or *He'll do this for me if he cares about me*. Extraordinary care in marriage is **mutual care**. That means both spouses want the other to be happy, and neither spouse wants the other to be unhappy. If you care about your spouse, you should never expect, or even accept, sacrifice as a solution to a problem.

A subtle form of sacrifice is the "I'll let you do what you want this time if you let me do what I want next time" solution. For example, if you want to go out with your friends after work, leaving your spouse with the children, you may suggest that you take the children another night so that your spouse can go out with his or her friends. But this isn't a win-win situation if one of you ends up unhappy whenever the other is happy. And once you've made this agreement, it can easily turn into a habit that pulls you apart.

Win-lose solutions are common in marriage because most couples don't understand how to arrive at win-win solutions. Their concept of fairness is that both spouses should suffer equally. But isn't it better to find solutions where neither spouse suffers? With a little creativity, you can find solutions that make both of you happy at the same time.

With both sacrifice and suffering out of the question, you're ready to brainstorm. And quantity is often more important than quality. So let your minds run wild; go with any thought that might satisfy both of you simultaneously. When you let your creative juices flow, you are more likely to find a lasting solution.

Take your notebooks with you throughout the day so you can enter possible solutions as they come to you. Modify your entries as you think of ways to improve upon them. Try to think outside the box. Come up with a long list of ways that you and your spouse might resolve the conflict with enthusiastic agreement.

### Guideline #4: Choose the solution that meets the conditions of the Policy of Joint Agreement—mutual and enthusiastic agreement.

After brainstorming, you'll have a list of both good and bad solutions. Good solutions are those both you and your spouse consider desirable. Bad solutions, on the other hand, take the feelings of one spouse into account at the expense of the other. The best solution is the one that makes you and your spouse most enthusiastic.

Many problems are relatively easy to solve if you know you must take each other's feelings into account. That's because you become aware of what it will take to reach a mutual agreement. Instead of considering options that clearly are not in your spouse's best interest, you think of options you know would make both you and your spouse happy.

Consider the problem we mentioned above. You would like to go out with your friends after work, leaving your spouse with the children. Before you followed the POJA, you may have simply called your spouse to say you'd be late, or worse yet, arrived home late without having called. But now you realize that if you want your spouse to be in love with you, you must come to an enthusiastic agreement prior to the event. It certainly restricts your freedom of choice, but on the other hand, it protects your spouse from your thoughtless behavior—and it safeguards your love for each other.

After having presented your case, you'd probably hear immediate objections. Your spouse might feel that he or she does not appreciate you having fun while he or she is home battling the kids. "Besides," your spouse might mention, "our leisure activities should be with each other." In response, you might suggest that your spouse drop the children off with your parents (whom *you* will call to make the arrangements) and join you.

If your spouse enthusiastically agrees, your conflict is resolved. Your parents take your children for a couple of hours, and your spouse joins you wherever it was you were planning to meet your friends. In fact, if going out after work with friends becomes a regular event, you can plan ahead for it by arranging the childcare in advance.

## Getting in Shape to Negotiate

Reading these four guidelines is the easy part. But putting them into practice will be a challenge for you. As I've said earlier, the democracy strategy is not easy. But it's the only one that actually resolves your conflicts and keeps you in love with each other.

So to help you start applying these guidelines to your conflicts, I suggest the following exercise. It will not require notebooks since each conflict will be rather simple. The purpose is to help you begin to think about each other when you can't agree.

Go to a grocery store together, without your children, and for about fifteen to thirty minutes find items for your cart that you would both be enthusiastic about buying. This shopping is to orient you to making mutually enjoyable choices, and you don't necessarily have to purchase your items when you are finished. I recommend grocery shopping for practice because there will be so many different choices that you are bound to find some that you would both enjoy.

Make sure that every item that goes in the cart is chosen with an enthusiastic agreement. The very act of asking each other how you feel regarding each item in question, and holding off on making a decision until you have agreement, is an extremely important habit to learn if you want to create a mutually enjoyable lifestyle.

It's perfectly okay to try to persuade each other by accepting an item on a trial basis. "Try it, you'll like it," is a legitimate negotiating strategy if one of you isn't sure how you would react to it. If your spouse is willing to try the item, take it home and taste it. If it's acceptable, add it to your cart the next time you practice. If not, leave it on the shelf. You can be enthusiastic about trying something that your spouse likes just to see how you would react to it. But if your enthusiasm disappears after sampling it, the trial should end.

When you think that you've gotten the hang of coming to an enthusiastic agreement about groceries, tackle some real conflicts you've been unable to resolve, this time using the notebooks I recommended. You'll probably be amazed at how quickly the POJA takes root.

## Practice Makes Perfect

If you follow the four guidelines I've suggested, negotiation can be an enjoyable way to learn about each other. And when you reach a solution that makes you both happy, you'll make substantial deposits into each other's Love Banks. In the end, the Policy of

Joint Agreement not only helps you become a great negotiator, it also protects your love for each other.

If you and your spouse have found yourselves acting more like dictators than sweethearts, it may sound overwhelming to switch to successful negotiations. The four guidelines may just seem like too much to remember.

But thankfully, once you establish the habit of negotiating with each other, it will be easy to run through the steps whenever there is a problem to solve. It's like learning to type. At first it seems impossible, but with practice it eventually becomes almost instinctive.

I often repeat a very accurate observation about my own marriage: Joyce and I have a conflict just about every hour we're together. But almost every conflict is resolved quickly and with enthusiastic agreement. Conflicts are to be expected when two people who are very different share life with each other. That being the case, knowing how to resolve these conflicts enjoyably and safely is absolutely essential to marital satisfaction.

By the time you become experts in finding win-win solutions to the problems you face, you will have learned what Joyce and I now know: we both need each other's perspective and judgment to have fulfillment in life.

---

In the second part of this book, I will be introducing five of the most common conflicts in marriage. As you read through the examples of how to go about resolving these conflicts, you will have an opportunity to practice negotiating with each other. And the more you practice, the easier and faster it will be to resolve other conflicts.

But before you begin learning how to resolve the five most common types of conflict in marriage, I'll introduce you to some important exceptions to following the Policy of Joint Agreement. While finding win-win solutions to marital conflicts should be your goal, there are some situations in which the default condition, doing nothing until an agreement is reached, can be unhealthy or even dangerous. In those situations, you must be able to protect yourself.

# 7

## Exceptions to the Rule

*N*ever *do anything without an enthusiastic agreement between you and your spouse.*

The Policy of Joint Agreement (POJA) is simply a rule to help couples remember that just about everything they do affects each other. And their wisest choices are those that take each other's feelings and interests into account. In other words, win-win outcomes in marital problem-solving are far superior to win-lose outcomes. The POJA reminds couples of that fact.

When a mutually enthusiastic agreement is reached, everyone would agree that a couple has discovered an ideal outcome. But anyone who has had a marital conflict knows all too well that enthusiastic agreements are often difficult to discover. And the default condition, never do anything, can sometimes have very unpleasant, if not disastrous, consequences.

With those dangerous consequences in mind, I recommend a sensible exception: the POJA should not be followed if doing nothing puts the health or safety of a spouse at risk. When a spouse is being subjected to physical or emotional abuse, infidelity, or abandonment, it makes no sense to follow this rule. Self-protection trumps thoughtfulness in those cases.

If a spouse is the victim of physical abuse, that spouse should report the abuse to authorities and separate for his or her own protection, even if the abusing spouse does not agree to that response. The same can be said in the case of infidelity or drug addiction. Some of the most effective ways to treat those problems and provide protection are usually opposed by the unfaithful or addicted spouse.

But in addition to health and safety issues, there is also another situation in marriage where a temporary suspension of the Policy of Joint Agreement can make sense: when you are trying to find a way to meet each other's most important emotional needs.

What should you do when your spouse has an emotional need that you are not enthusiastic about meeting? Does the POJA get you off the hook? Or are you obligated to meet each other's important emotional needs even if you are not enthusiastic about it?

The answers to these questions are found in understanding the purpose of the Policy of Joint Agreement. It's a rule to help you resolve conflicts with mutual care and consideration. The default condition, don't do anything, is not designed to be a permanent solution to any marital problem. It is what you do while you are trying to discover a solution.

If you've read my book *His Needs, Her Needs*, you already know that I put a great deal of emphasis on spouses meeting each other's most important emotional needs. Failing to do so should not be an option in marriage. But I also emphasize the importance of meeting each other's emotional needs with mutual enthusiastic agreement. So what should a spouse do when he or she does not enjoy meeting an emotional need? The solution may require doing something reluctantly on a trial basis as part of a plan to find an enjoyable outcome. But the trial should not persist very long. Either it should show promise almost immediately, or the couple should go back to brainstorming for other methods.

I once had a job stuffing envelopes. It was such a mundane and repetitive task that at first I could hardly wait until it was finished. But when the project ended after about three weeks, I actually missed the job. I had modified my envelope-stuffing technique until I did it quickly and almost effortlessly. And I had also made friends with my associates while we worked together. In fact, I was able to figure out how to enjoy most of the jobs I had while in college.

The same thing can be true in learning how to meet emotional needs. Let's take sex and conversation as examples. Most men have a craving for sex, and most women have a craving for affection and conversation. Men can't understand why their wives would give up an opportunity to have sex. *What's so tough about making love?* And their wives wonder why their husbands resist being affectionate and talking to them. *What's so exhausting about giving me a hug and talking to me for a while?*

The problem, of course, is that men and women differ in what they enjoy most. It's not that women never enjoy sex or that men never enjoy affection and conversation. It's just that they don't usually enjoy it as much.

So if a wife is not enthusiastic about having sex with a husband who is craving it, should she violate the POJA to meet his need? And what about a wife who needs her husband's affection and conversation? Should he try to meet her need even when he doesn't feel like doing it? Is the spouse who wants their emotional needs met at all costs being selfish and uncaring?

The problem with violations of the POJA in meeting emotional needs goes beyond the issue of selfishness—one spouse gaining at the other's expense. It also inhibits the ability of the reluctant spouse to meet that emotional need in the future. The less you enjoy doing something, the less likely you'll do it again. If a husband or wife want their emotional needs met often, their spouse must do it with enthusiasm. They must enjoy doing something that they don't crave in the same way. They must learn to do what I did, to enjoy stuffing envelopes when I didn't have a need to do it.

## How to Enjoy Meeting an Emotional Need That You Don't Have

There are two primary motivators in life. The most powerful is to enjoy doing something, and the next most powerful is to enjoy its consequences—the closer to doing it the better.

So whether the desired behavior is sex, affection, or conversation, if one spouse does not have a very strong emotional need for it, it's incumbent on the other spouse to be sure that it's enjoyable and that its consequences are enjoyable. Otherwise, the spouse with the lesser need will come up with a host of excuses to avoid it.

Suppose your spouse wants sex and you are too tired to even think about it. Should you meet your spouse's need even if it violates the rule, or should you wait until you are enthusiastic about doing it?

As I mentioned in the last chapter, you can be enthusiastic about trying something new to see if it might be an enjoyable solution to a problem. It's the "try it, you'll like it" approach to resolving conflicts. But would having sex when you can hardly stay awake be part of that temporary plan? I doubt it. It's more likely that it would be a way of getting your spouse to stop bothering you or to stop trying to make you feel guilty.

If you were to help your spouse understand what you enjoy most about making love, and the conditions that are most favorable for you, you may agree to try making love that way for a while. You may also suggest that after making love, your spouse meet your emotional needs, such as conversation and affection, as an enjoyable consequence for you.

At first, your offer may not be carried out exactly as planned. Your spouse may need to have a better understanding of what it takes to make it enjoyable for you. And the affection and conversation that follow may need improvement. So you wouldn't necessarily be enjoying the process that much. But if your spouse were to eventually meet all your conditions, you'd find yourself as enthusiastic about making love as your spouse.

The goal should be to eventually meet each other's important emotional needs with mutual enthusiastic agreement. But the path to that final outcome may temporarily require you to be less than happy as you are trying to discover the best way to meet each other's needs.

Spouses have difficulty meeting each other's emotional needs when they have not been motivated. They don't enjoy meeting those needs, and they don't enjoy the consequences of meeting them.

Such reasoning is insulting to many spouses. *Why should I reward my spouse for making love to me? Or having a conversation with me? Or being affectionate with me? If my spouse really cares about me, wouldn't he or she want to meet my needs without being rewarded?*

Can you see how that way of thinking will make it harder for you to meet each other's emotional needs, regardless of how caring you might be? Short-term sacrifice to reach long-term mutual enjoyment makes sense. But unless your ultimate plan is to create mutual enjoyment and mutual reward, your plan will not work. Temporary sacrifice will turn into permanent sacrifice. And that will lead to an aversion to meeting each other's emotional needs. You will hate the very thought of it.

What are the best rewards for meeting each other's emotional needs? It's meeting each other's emotional needs. If one of you has a craving for sex and the other has a craving for affection and conversation, combine them. Make sex the reward for affection and conversation. Make affection and conversation the reward for sex.

Another essential consideration is how you make love and express your affection, and what you talk about. The one with the lowest need should be given preference because if your need is to be met, you must make the experience as enjoyable as possible to the one meeting that need.

In most cases, it's the wife who has the lowest need for sex, and the husband who has the lowest need for affection and conversation. So if the husband wants more sex, and the wife wants more affection and conversation, they must both commit themselves to meeting those needs, which may mean a temporary violation of the POJA. But during that trial period, it's incumbent upon the spouse with the greater need to learn to make the experience enjoyable to the spouse with the lesser need. When they have it figured out, they will be meeting each other's emotional needs with enthusiastic agreement.

When you find yourselves failing to meet each other's emotional needs, don't let another week go by without addressing this problem. Think of a plan that will lead to a solution. Remember that if you want your emotional needs to be met, your spouse must come to enjoy meeting those needs and be rewarded for doing so. Don't get bogged down with the illusion that your spouse owes it to you, or that you shouldn't have to consider rewards. And also remember that if meeting your needs is at all unpleasant, that's the quickest way to squelch your spouse's willingness to meet them.

# PART 2

# Resolving Common Marital Conflicts with Negotiation

Now that you've learned the goal and rules of effective marital negotiation, you're ready to address some of the most common conflicts that married couples face. If you resolve them the right way, with win-win outcomes, your lifestyle will be enjoyable and your love for each other will grow. But if you resolve them the wrong way, with win-lose outcomes, your lifestyle will be very disappointing—and you'll wonder what it was that you ever saw in each other.

I can't put too much emphasis on the fact that the way you resolve these and other marital conflicts will determine whether your marriage will be a success or a failure. By addressing each of these five common conflicts using the negotiating strategy I've introduced to you, you will not only be approaching these problems the right way (with respect and mutual understanding), but you are also more likely to find the wisest solutions possible.

In the following five chapters, I will not only encourage you to practice resolving your conflicts the right way, but I will also describe some of the differences I've observed in the perspectives of husbands and wives when these conflicts arise. You will either respect and accommodate these differences in a final resolution that solves the problem once and for all, or you will be disrespectful and ignore them, leaving the problem unresolved. The choice is yours.

# 8

## Conflicts over Friends and Relatives

The Policy of Joint Agreement forces a couple to put each other first—to make each other their highest priority. So when there's a conflict over friends and relatives, the POJA makes each spouse's interests more important than the interests of any friend or relative. No one can come between a husband and wife that follow the Policy of Joint Agreement, and that helps guarantee a couple's love for each other. But it also seems difficult to justify at times.

A few years ago, I spoke to a group of couples from China about what it took to maintain romantic love in marriage. I needed a translator because most of the audience could not speak or understand English. After my speech, I took questions from the audience, and one was particularly insightful. The question came from an older woman who felt threatened by the POJA. She asked, "If my son follows the Policy of Joint Agreement, would he not be putting his wife's interests above those of his parents? It is our custom to serve our parents above all else."

China is not the only culture that puts the interests of parents above those of a spouse. It's common throughout the world. But even where that value is not outwardly stated, it's very difficult to ignore. People often assume responsibility to parents that can override their responsibility to their spouse.

That same kind of thinking can apply to siblings and possibly even to extended family members—if any of them are in trouble, we will be there to give them a helping hand even if our spouse were to object. Or consider friends you've known since childhood who may have helped you at a time of great personal need. After all, isn't that what friends are for: to help and support each other?

Given our sense of responsibility to our family and friends, along with our enjoyment of their company, the following question almost invariably comes up after marriage: *What do I do when I face a conflict with my spouse over friends and relatives?*

If a member of your family or a friend needs your help, should you be there for them even if you don't have your spouse's enthusiastic agreement? If your mother cannot care for herself and wants you to care for her, possibly in your own home, should you provide that care even if your spouse considers it to be an invasion of your privacy? If one of your friends is about to move and that friend has helped you move in the past, should you help your friend even if your spouse would prefer that you spend the weekend at home with your family? If you simply want to relax and have a good time with your best friends, should your spouse have the right to ruin it all by objecting? And what if one of those best friends happens to be of the opposite sex? Should you abandon that friendship forever just because your spouse is jealous?

Those are tough questions, and in many cases they come up in situations that require answers almost instantly. When one of these conflicts arises, you usually don't have the luxury of days or weeks of negotiation with your spouse. So take some time now, while you can carefully think it through, to resolve some of the conflicts that you may be having now, or in the future, over friends and relatives.

## Reviewing Your Options

In this book, we've discussed five marital problem-solving strategies. I called the first approach the **sacrifice strategy**. It's voluntarily letting your spouse win while you lose as an act of care. Your husband wants to invite his parents over to your house for dinner. You would rather spend the evening doing something together as a family, like riding bikes, but as an act of care for your spouse you agree. You are upset about having to get a special dinner ready on such short notice, but you don't let on because that would spoil your husband's fun. And the next time your husband wants his parents over for dinner, you agree to it again.

The sacrifice strategy is very common while dating and early in marriage. But it doesn't take a couple long before they realize that sacrifice eventually becomes both expected and unappreciated. Lifestyle decisions based on sacrifice backfire.

A second option is the **dictator strategy**. It's the use of demands, disrespect, and anger to try to force your spouse to do what you want even when it's not in your spouse's best interest to do so. Your spouse tells you that his parents will be coming over for dinner (selfish demand). If you object, he blames your reluctance on an uncaring attitude (disrespectful judgment). And finally, when all else fails, he raises his voice, stomps from room to room, and throws things around until he gets his way (angry outburst). If you're too tired or too afraid to argue, you give in and prepare dinner.

Another strategy that is similar to the dictator strategy is the **dueling dictators strategy**. Spouses who both struggle for control use this approach. Instead of merely objecting to your husband's dinner invitation to his parents, you make a demand of your own: *Tell your parents that we have decided to spend the evening going on a bike ride together as a family.* Your children, upon hearing this, run up to you begging to go on that bike ride. When your husband says, *No, your grandma and grandpa will be joining us for dinner,* the fight begins. With your children siding with you, and you telling your husband that his parents are more important to him than his own children (disrespectful judgment), you both start screaming at each other (angry outburst). The children run for cover.

The dictator and dueling dictators strategies are not the right way to go about resolving marital conflicts, and most couples who fight know it. Those strategies not only fail to help them resolve their conflicts, but they destroy the love they have for each other. So when spouses find that they only make matters worse, they try another approach. They use the **anarchy strategy**: *If you don't enjoy having dinner with my parents, I'll go out to dinner with them by myself.* And you respond, *Fine! The children and I will go on our bike ride without you.* It's not mutual agreement, but rather a unilateral choice that is sprung on a spouse with little or no notice. This strategy leads to marital alienation that will cause the couple to eventually lose their emotional bond. Instead of being lovers, partners, and best friends in life, they become ships passing in the night.

The fifth approach to marital problem solving, the **democracy strategy**, is the only one that actually resolves marital conflict to the satisfaction of both spouses. It helps find solutions that strengthen a couple's emotional bond and builds romantic love for each other. When you use this strategy, you're making your spouse an equal partner in deciding how to resolve any conflicts that may appear by following the Policy of Joint Agreement (making a final decision only after you both agree to it enthusiastically).

This democracy strategy begins with the first of our Four Guidelines to Successful Negotiation: you guarantee each other a pleasant and safe discussion by being cheerful and by avoiding demands, disrespectful judgments, and angry outbursts. If either of you cannot make that guarantee, you postpone the discussion until you can.

The second guideline is to introduce what it is you want, and learn how your spouse would feel about fulfilling your request. You tell your spouse that you would like to invite your parents over for dinner, without having discussed it with them first. Then you ask your spouse how he or she would feel about it, letting your spouse reveal any objections without countering with disrespect.

With your request on the table and your spouse's objections understood, you are ready for the third guideline—brainstorming. Your goal is to reach an enthusiastic agreement regarding having your parents over for the evening. So under what conditions would your spouse be enthusiastic about that? What are some of the ways that you could have your parents over without having to cook a meal and clean up after a busy day at work?

Finally, you're ready for the fourth guideline. You come to an enthusiastic agreement or you continue to brainstorm. If you can't agree in time for the event, no invitation is given—you don't invite your parents over. But your final decision may be to invite your parents to join your family in a bike ride instead of dinner. It would set a precedent for future invitations if it worked out well for both of you.

The illustration I've used here regarding having parents over for dinner is a fairly easy conflict to resolve with enthusiastic agreement. We're assuming, of course, that your parents are delightful to entertain. But what happens when your spouse simply doesn't want to get anywhere near your parents? Perhaps your parents are disrespectful or downright cruel to your spouse. If he or she feels obligated to be with your unpleasant parents, you risk making Love Bank withdrawals every time he or she even thinks about them.

If you follow the POJA from the beginning of your marriage onward, that won't happen. Neither spouse is obligated to spend time with people who make them unhappy because of the default condition (do nothing until an enthusiastic agreement is reached). You can't force your parents to treat your wife with respect, but you don't have to spend time with them, either. If you resolve this conflict the right way, your parents will come to realize that they won't be seeing much of either of you until they change their ways.

The Policy of Joint Agreement helps form and reshape your relationships with friends and relatives to satisfy both of you. Unless they treat both of you thoughtfully and respectfully, and you enjoy their company, you shouldn't make them a part of your lives.

## Men and Women Interpret Relationships with Friends and Relatives Differently

Don't be surprised if you and your spouse have different perspectives when it comes to friends and relatives. When a conflict arises, you may notice that you don't always agree on how to deal with it because of the way you look at the situation.

Remember what I said earlier about the corpus callosum, the band of fibers that connects the neurons of the left and right hemispheres of the brain? In a woman's brain, it's much thicker, which means that there are many more fibers. Their brains are much more interconnected. From a functional standpoint, that means women have the capacity to take more information into account when they make decisions. A wife might want more recreational time to be spent with their children and would also be concerned about everyone in the family getting enough exercise every day. So a family bike ride after dinner would be just the ticket. Her husband, who had a brief conversation with his mom and dad that day, couldn't see why having them over for dinner would be a problem. For him, it was a simple matter of having them included in a meal that was already scheduled.

This example resonates with Joyce and me. Prior to our marriage, my friends and I would get together impulsively. I'd show up at their house and they would show up at mine without formal invitation. My door was always open to my friends and theirs were open to me. I thought I was being particularly thoughtful in dating Joyce by giving her a one-hour notice that I'd be over to take her out for the evening.

So imagine my surprise after marriage when Joyce didn't want my friends coming over uninvited. In fact, she didn't even want me to invite them unless she first agreed to have them come. For me, having a friend over was nothing but fun. If we wanted privacy, we simply wouldn't answer the door. But for Joyce, even having her own friends over was work. She had to clean the house, prepare something to eat, and plan games for the evening. For me, none of that mattered.

It's the differences in our brains that were at the root of our conflict. She imagined what the entire evening would be like, and I didn't give it much thought.

We often have a similar conflict when preparing for a trip. Joyce methodically goes through every day we'll be gone and plans precisely what she will be wearing each day with a few extra options just in case. On the other hand, I like to throw a few clothes into the suitcase an hour before we leave. Joyce plans for the future while I take it as it comes.

Depending on your perspective, and whether you're male or female, you will see value in either Joyce's approach or my approach to inviting friends over. Each one has its advantages and disadvantages. For us, the conflict was resolved by developing an entirely new set of friends. The impulsive singles that had been my friends prior to marriage were replaced by couples we both enjoyed and with whom we had more in common. As is the case with most couples, they didn't just show up—they had to be invited before coming to spend the evening with us. And I didn't show up at their house without an invitation. I learned to plan our evenings with friends more carefully, but Joyce also eased up on the conditions she felt were necessary.

You might think that I gave up on the way I enjoyed having friends over and that Joyce had to put up with a more chaotic way to spend evenings. But that's not what happened. We both enjoyed our new friends, and we both enjoyed the way we spent time with them. We were invited to other couples' homes far more often than we had been to the homes of my single friends. And Joyce and I worked together when we had friends over. We became partners in choosing our friends and partners in the way we entertained them. It turned out to be a far wiser solution than what either of us alone would have considered to be appropriate.

## It Pays to Be Prepared

Because many of the decisions you make regarding the care of your parents or friends have to be made instantly, you and your spouse should discuss many of these issues before they actually arise. For example, if your parents or your spouse's parents were to require your care, what kind of care could you provide with an enthusiastic agreement? Neither one of you should feel pressured into making an agreement that is not actually in your own best interest. So now is the time for you to start thinking about what kind of care you can provide and how long that care should continue.

What would you do if a friend needed help moving? Or if a friend invited you both out to dinner? Or if a friend invited one of you out to dinner but didn't invite the other? Or if the friend had been a former lover?

Trust me. Former lovers should be left completely out of your lives. But what about friends of the opposite sex in general? How friendly do you really want these relationships to be? I have warned couples for years that most affairs begin with opposite-sex friendships that start out innocently. Are you willing to risk an affair by developing a good friendship with someone of the opposite sex? In most cases, your opposite-sex friendships that are the most dangerous will make your spouse uncomfortable. You will not have your spouse's enthusiastic agreement when you try to get together with those friends, or even have casual communication via social networking sites, email, or texting.

The Policy of Joint Agreement forces you and your spouse to negotiate fairly with each other, and it keeps you focused on each other's best interests even when you reject each other's proposed options. It keeps you thoughtful when you're tempted to be selfish. If you follow the POJA, your family and friends will never come between you.

Get into the habit of discussing all invitations with your spouse before responding. When somebody invites you, say to them, "Let me get back to you after I've discussed it with my spouse." Your family and friends will get used to the idea that you make your decisions together.

Don't let friends and relatives destroy your love for each other. When conflicts pit the interests of your spouse against those of your friends and relatives, he or she should always be your highest priority. Your spouse is your most important friend and relative. No other should ever be allowed to come between you. Follow the Policy of Joint Agreement and Four Guidelines for Successful Negotiation to make sure they don't.

## Consider This . . .

1. What are five strategies to resolving conflicts over friends and relatives? Why should you always avoid four of them and learn to become experts at using the fifth?

2. Think of a conflict you have over friends and relatives. If you used the first strategy to resolving conflicts that I describe in this chapter, how would you try to resolve it? If you used the second strategy, what would you do? How about using the third or fourth strategies? Why would all four of these strategies for marital problem solving diminish the love you have for each other?

3. Use the fifth approach I suggested to help you resolve the conflict you discussed in question #2. Remember to use a notebook to help guide your discussion (refer to appendix A as an example).

4. Try to anticipate some of the conflicts you may have with family and friends. If your parents or your spouse's parents

were to require your care, what kind of care could you provide with an enthusiastic agreement? Where will you be spending Christmas? What would you do if a friend needed help moving? What if a friend invited you both out to dinner? Or if a friend invited one of you out to dinner, but didn't invite the other? Or if the friend had been a former lover? Think of other situations with family and friends that might lead to conflict in the future. How will you handle these situations so that you'll have an enthusiastic agreement?

# 9

## Conflicts over Career Requirements and Time Management

Everything you do throughout the day makes either deposits or withdrawals in each other's Love Banks. That's why it's so important to decide what you will be doing before you do it. And that decision should be made with enthusiastic agreement if you want to maximize Love Bank deposits and minimize withdrawals.

But how can you have a mutually enthusiastic agreement about your daily schedule when you have enlisted in the army and have just been assigned to a year's tour of duty? Or when you're on call at a hospital for emergency care? Or when you work for an airline that assigns you to a travel schedule? The requirements of a career will usually trump the Policy of Joint Agreement when it comes to how you schedule your time.

Marital conflict over a career usually has more to do with the way the career dominates a time schedule than its other aspects. Some careers are so flexible regarding time schedules that the interests of a marriage can be easily accommodated. But other careers are notoriously damaging to marriages because of the time constraints they impose. This is especially true when a career separates a couple or prevents them from having enough time to meet each other's emotional needs.

If your spouse is unhappy with what your career requires you to do, you're making Love Bank withdrawals every time you go to work. You may think that when it comes to earning a living, you don't have any choices. Your spouse simply must learn to adjust to your career's demands. But after complaining about it for a while, your spouse is likely to adjust by becoming emotionally disconnected from you so that the effects of the career don't hurt as much. In other words, your spouse will simply fall out of love with you.

Take it from me, a seasoned veteran when it comes to changing people: *it's much easier to change a behavior than it is to change an emotional reaction to a behavior.* If you tell your spouse not to feel the way he or she does when you do something, you're making a terrible mistake because your spouse's reactions are very unlikely to change. On the other hand, if you change your behavior to produce a positive reaction instead of a negative one in your spouse, that reaction will also persist as long as you continue your new behavior.

If your work schedule or career requirements make your spouse unhappy, change them. And if necessary, create a new career that gives you enough flexibility to keep your marriage healthy and happy.

When I introduce this idea of changing careers to couples, many of them think I'm being unrealistic. And yet when you consider the career paths of most people, they usually change several times during a person's lifetime. One way or another, you are likely to have at least one new career during your lifetime. Are you willing to change your career path out of consideration for your spouse, or will you let some of the random factors of life make those changes for you?

Your career should support your spouse and family, not the other way around. Its primary purpose is to provide a satisfying lifestyle. But what if the career itself causes you or your spouse to lose your love for each other? Then the career is defeating its very purpose. Instead of creating a comfortable lifestyle, it's creating a miserable lifestyle, at least for your spouse.

Some people have tried to argue that their career choice is a personal decision. Since it's something that they will be doing most of their waking hours, the first and foremost consideration should be whether or not they like doing it. People who use this argument are usually afraid that their spouse will force them into a career that they really don't want.

But the Policy of Joint Agreement handles that problem. It requires both of you to be enthusiastic about your final decision. It guides you to a career that you will enjoy because that's one of the conditions that must be met.

If you follow the conditions of the POJA, when your negotiations are over you will have a career that's just as fulfilling as the one you have now, if not more so. And your spouse will be as enthusiastic about it as you are.

## Is Your Schedule Destroying Your Love?

Is your schedule, particularly your work schedule, any of your spouse's business? Do you resent any attempt by your spouse to change an appointment or business trip that he or she finds objectionable?

If you don't think that your schedule is your spouse's business, your love for each other doesn't have much hope. That's because it plays such an important role in the way spouses care for each other. When you make scheduling decisions over the objections of your spouse, you are offering positive proof that you care more about your job than you care about your spouse.

I've heard many arguments about how unreasonable a spouse's objections are. "If I were to do what my wife wants me to do, we'd lose everything. She doesn't understand how much commitment it takes to support the family." It takes commitment, all right. But is it commitment to support the family or commitment to support a job?

Has your work schedule become a higher priority than your care for your spouse? There's an easy way to determine the answer. Ask your spouse how he or she feels about your schedule. If your spouse is unhappy with anything you've planned, are you willing to change that plan to accommodate his or her feelings? If the answer is no, your schedule is more important than your care for your spouse. You're not working to make your spouse happy because the way you're working fails to achieve that objective. Your career fulfillment comes at your spouse's expense.

## How to Create a Mutually Enthusiastic Schedule

If you want to have a schedule that helps you make Love Bank deposits instead of withdrawals, you must negotiate with each other. I suggest that every Sunday afternoon you meet to discuss your schedules for the coming week. No time should be spent on any activity, including work, unless first agreed to enthusiastically.

Everything planned for the entire week should be approved by both of you before it can be enacted. Literally every hour should be spent doing what you have agreed to do. If, during the week, a change in schedule is requested by either of you, you must both enthusiastically agree to the change for it to take effect.

The first time you attempt to complete this assignment, it won't be easy. You may have become so accustomed to making your schedule independently of your spouse's input that you will have great difficulty negotiating at first. So I suggest that you set aside several hours, or even a weekend, for your first negotiating session.

One of my cardinal rules for couples is to schedule a minimum of fifteen hours each week to meet each other's intimate emotional needs. During that time you are to be affectionate, talk to each other, enjoy recreational activities together, and make love (see *His Needs, Her Needs*). So make sure that your schedule includes this time for undivided attention. Don't let a week go by without giving each other the attention you need to make the most Love Bank deposits possible.

Another high priority is the time you spend together as a family. I call it quality family time, and unless it's carefully scheduled, it won't happen. Other, less important activities will crowd it out of your lives.

I've spoken to many people who are close to death, and none of them have ever told me they should have spent more time at work. If people have regret later in life, it's that they didn't spend more time with their spouse and children.

As you plan your week together, you'll find that you won't have time for everything you want to do. But if you schedule it ahead of time, and follow your schedule, you will accomplish what is most important to both of you.

## Men and Women Interpret Career Requirements and Time Management Differently

In general, wives want their husbands to spend more time with them and their children. They resent careers that separate them. That's because women appear to have an instinct for the importance of a father being an integrated part of the family unit. They also seem to have an understanding of how their time together is essential for emotional bonding. A wife is usually the first to know when a marital relationship is in trouble.

A husband, on the other hand, often doesn't see how his schedule affects the quality of his marriage. His schedule is not only filled with career requirements, but also with personal recreational activities, hobbies, the internet, church responsibilities, fitness programs, and a host of other interests that take his time and attention away from his wife and family.

At first, a wife makes a valiant effort to work out a schedule that brings their lives together. But when it becomes apparent that her husband wants to go it alone, she gives up and follows her own interests without him. It doesn't take her long, however, to discover that their independent lifestyles are leading to marital disaster. She knows that they are growing apart.

A few years ago, I counseled a couple who was about to divorce. The wife said that she could no longer live with a husband who spent his weekends golfing and was never willing to include her in his recreational interests. I encouraged him to find another activity that he could enjoy with her, but he was adamantly opposed to changing his golfing routine. Then he hurt his back and was unable to golf for about a year. During that time, he discovered new activities that he could share with his wife, and today they are happily married—without golf.

Spouses can live happily without careers and activities that ruin their marriage. Why wait for chance events to do it for you when you can make the decision now?

I planned my career with my wife in mind. Joyce was uncomfortable with my first and second career choices because she felt they would adversely affect our time together. But we finally agreed on a profession that allowed me the flexibility in my schedule to be an integrated part of her life: psychology.

It would have been pointless for me to start my career development without her enthusiastic agreement. After all, my career was to be a joint effort with joint compensation. Without her support, the career would not serve our mutual purposes in life. Her encouragement has made my choice particularly satisfying and undoubtedly accounts for much of its success.

Joyce's career choices were also made with the same consideration for my interests. So throughout our lives together, I have supported her career as enthusiastically as she has supported mine. I consider her work as a gospel singer and radio host/producer to be an effort we make jointly. I never resent the time she spends pursuing her career, because she is willing to accommodate my interests with her schedule and choice of career activities.

Since we are both ambitious people, our careers could have wrecked our marriage. They could have driven us in opposite directions. But instead, our careers have strengthened our marriage, because we consider each other more important than our work. Our deep love for each other is the result.

Don't lose your love for each other due to neglect. Every Sunday afternoon, make a date to review your schedules for the coming week. Use the Policy of Joint Agreement and the Four Guidelines to Successful Negotiation to try to resolve any conflicts you may have as you are putting your schedule together. Also, don't forget to include fifteen hours for undivided attention so that you can meet each other's emotional needs for affection, sexual fulfillment, intimate conversation, and recreational companionship. And also include time for you to be together as a family. Your influence over your children is greatest when you take time to be with them.

Each of you brings a valuable perspective to every decision you will make in life. But when it comes to time management, I tend to find a wife's perspective particularly important because it recognizes the value of time together in marriage. Women usually have a keen sense for what it takes to make a marital relationship work, and what they want most is their husband's undivided attention.

The careers you both choose, and the way you schedule your time, should always be carried out with each other in mind. Make your career and schedule Love Builders, not Love Busters.

## Consider This . . .

1. Have you been demanding, disrespectful, or angry when you've discussed your career responsibilities or time schedules with each other? Have you used any excuses for these abusive tactics to try to justify them?

2. Instead of arguing about your career responsibilities or time schedule, do you simply do what you think is right and hope that your spouse will adjust to it? What is the likely outcome when a spouse is expected to adjust to a decision that has not been enthusiastically accepted?

3. When does a career responsibility or a time schedule become a Love Buster? Do either of you feel you have the right to make decisions about your career or schedule independently of the other's interests and feelings? Are you willing to give

up that right by following the POJA for the sake of your love for each other?

4. Careers are not the only obstacle to time schedule agreement. Are recreational activities, hobbies, the internet, church responsibilities, fitness programs, or other interests crowding out the time you should spend together? Each of these should either occur with your mutual enthusiastic agreement or be eliminated from your lifestyle.

# 10

## Conflicts over Financial Management

Financial conflicts can go on endlessly in marriage unless you establish basic guidelines. Those guidelines are called a budget, and every household should have one. So before wandering into the trees of specific financial issues, let's first step back to see the forest. I strongly encourage you to create a budget before you face the myriad of individual financial issues.

But I don't want you to create just any budget. I want you to create one with the Policy of Joint Agreement as your guide. When it's completed, you'll have come a long way toward resolving one of the most common types of conflict in marriage—financial conflict. A budget helps you determine in advance what you expect to earn and how you plan to spend it. When you come to an enthusiastic agreement regarding that plan, and then follow it, very few individual financial conflicts emerge because you've settled them in advance.

So the first step in learning how to resolve conflicts over financial management is to create a budget that you can agree to enthusiastically. If you have never created a formal budget to determine how your income is to be spent, you should begin with a household budget form that is readily available in bookstores or online. It should contain at least seventy categories of income and household expenses.

You may download free of charge the budget form I've written if you wish. It's in the questionnaires section of the Marriage Builders.com website under the title "Financial Support Inventory: Needs and Wants Budget." As you'll discover, though, it does more than just help you create a budget. It also helps you meet the need for financial support.

## The Anatomy of a Budget

A budget has two basic parts: the income section and the expenses section. The income section of the budget is usually the easiest part to agree upon, especially if it's a fixed amount. But if your income changes from month to month, there may be some conflict over whether to estimate your income optimistically or pessimistically. I suggest that you use a low estimate with a contingency plan for how to spend money earned over that amount. That way you're covered if your income is not as much as you had hoped it would be, but you also have a plan for how to spend any extra income you receive. Include all income before any payroll deductions and then show those deductions as an expense.

Then comes the hard part. Where is that income to be spent? If you are like most couples, you are not earning as much money as you would like to spend, and each of you will have different priorities.

So I recommend that each of you complete your own copy of the budget first so you can be aware of the conflicts that exist (e.g., one of you would like to spend a thousand dollars for Christmas gifts and the other feels that two hundred dollars should be sufficient). The budgets must balance, so your initial budgets should not have you spending more than you've earned. They should also include current commitments. What are essential costs and what are discretionary costs? Once-a-year expenses, like insurance and Christmas gifts, should be prorated each month so that the funds will be there to pay them when they come due.

After you have your two budgets to compare, you are ready to discuss all conflicts that you find. How will you reconcile them?

First, remind each other that your conversation must be pleasant and safe if you are to come to an enthusiastic agreement. And also remind each other that the default position on the Policy of Joint Agreement is to do nothing. If you can't come to an enthusiastic agreement, the money for that category should remain in your checking account unless you can arrive at a temporary agreement you can both accept enthusiastically.

Second, discover each other's opinions about the issue respectfully to understand what kind of a solution would work for both of you. Granted, there are some who simply don't want to spend any money—they're tightwads. The default condition, not doing anything, is precisely what they want. I'll address that problem in chapter 16. But most couples try to find common ground when they respect each other's perspectives.

The third step is to brainstorm—think of solutions that might make both of you happy. If you can't think of anything immediately, let the problem incubate for a day or two, and then come back to it again. It's amazing what your brain can do when you give it a chance to process information for a while.

Finally, take the fourth step by finding a solution that you can both agree to enthusiastically. Again, I want to remind you why

I want you to find enthusiastic agreements as opposed to reluctant agreements. Enthusiastic agreements create a lifestyle that deposits love units in both of your Love Banks, while reluctant agreements create one that makes withdrawals for at least the spouse who is reluctant. If you want to be in love, don't settle for reluctant agreements.

You will find that your enthusiastic agreements regarding your budget will set a standard for financial decisions in the future. While reluctant agreements must be renegotiated every time a conflict arises, an enthusiastic agreement usually ends further discussion. You will know what to do whenever the problem arises. Enthusiastic agreements may take longer to discover than reluctant agreements, but they lead to far less negotiating overall. And as your negotiating skills improve, when new financial conflicts arise you will be able to resolve most of them very quickly.

## Men and Women Interpret the Goals of Financial Management Differently

When one spouse makes financial decisions without accommodating the perspective of the other, love units are lost. It's that simple. But when financial decisions are made with the feelings of both spouses in mind, it's a wiser plan that also builds the feeling of love.

So if you want to be wise and build your love for each other, you should have a budget that takes the interests and feelings of both of you into account. Every item in that budget should be subject to mutual enthusiastic agreement, and you should stick to what you've agreed to do unless you want to reopen budgetary negotiation.

But in making that budget, you'll probably find that your priorities will be different. In general, women want their limited financial resources to be spent for security, while men want it spent for enjoyment. The wife may want to spend more on the support and care of the family than the husband does, while the husband may want to spend more on recreational interests than his wife does.

Since few of us have the resources to buy everything we would like to have, there comes a time in every couple's life when priorities must be set. And the conflicting financial goals of a husband and wife can make coming to an enthusiastic agreement on every budget item very difficult.

If you face a conflict over how to budget your income, begin with the assumption that there is some truth in both of your perspectives. The wife who wants the budget to support the security of the family is defending a very important value. But so is the husband who wants the budget to cover recreational expenses. It's not an either-or issue. You should want to find how both can be achieved.

## What If She Has an Emotional Need for Financial Support?

As I mentioned earlier, you are welcome to download our free Needs and Wants Budget. But as soon as you see it, you will notice that it suggests a different approach to budgeting than the one I just outlined, which simply guides you to a fair budget agreement. The Needs and Wants Budget does more. It's designed to meet a wife's need for financial support.

Whether you decide to simply find agreement on a fair budget or one that meets her need for financial support (but is also fair) will depend on whether or not one of her most important emotional needs is financial support. That can be determined by completing the Emotional Needs Questionnaire found in appendix B and also in the questionnaires section of the Marriage Builders.com website.

If you discover that she has a need for financial support, I encourage the wife to complete the first draft of the budget that I call the Needs Budget. Only the husband's income is to be included in that first draft. I make that recommendation for a very important reason. If a woman has an emotional need for financial support, when her husband supports her and their children financially, he makes considerable deposits into her Love Bank. By completing the first draft of the budget using only his income, she is able to express precisely how she would like that need for financial support to be met by him. When a husband's income covers the amounts she lists in the Needs Budget, by definition he meets her need for financial support.

When a man first hears of this recommendation, he often thinks that his wife will be writing the entire budget. There will be nothing left for anything he needs. What happened to the Policy of Joint Agreement?

But in the many years that I have encouraged couples to follow this procedure, I have yet to find a wife who made her budgetary requirements unreasonable or completely out of reach of her husband. And it gives him plenty of opportunity to negotiate for what he would like to buy. Remember, this is the first draft, not the final budget.

After the Needs Budget is completed by the wife, both husband and wife add expenses to the next draft, the Wants Budget. These are expenses that the husband feels he needs that have not been included in the first draft, as well as other things he might want. Since the wife has already expressed her needs, she adds her wants to this second draft. And this time, her income is included.

Now comes the negotiating. If you are like almost all other couples, your needs and wants will far outstrip your joint income. So you should both agree enthusiastically on the final draft, which I call the Affordable Budget.

Put special emphasis on trying to include the expenses that the wife wrote into the first draft. And make sure that the husband's income covers those expenses. If that cannot be achieved with enthusiastic agreement, it means that her emotional need for financial support is not being met with your new budget. It also means that you should focus your attention on how that need can be met in the future. In *His Needs, Her Needs*, the companion to this book, I explain (in chapter 9—Financial Support) how important it is to meet a wife's need for financial support, and how that can be achieved with enthusiastic agreement.

But if the wife's need for financial support as described in the Needs Budget is covered by the husband's income, the remainder of the budget process is a matter of reconciling what remains of his income, and her income, with expenses that they both would like to add.

The final product, the Affordable Budget, may take you a while to finalize. In the meantime, remember the default condition of the POJA: Don't spend anything until you both agree to it enthusiastically. If you can't come to an agreement within a few weeks, find a mediator to help you think of creative alternatives.

One more cautionary remark is in order. Just because you've hammered out a budget with enthusiastic agreement doesn't mean that you'll be enthusiastic about it once it's implemented. The Policy of Joint Agreement applies to everything you do, but what you plan to do may not turn out the way you expected. You may be very unenthusiastic about the result. So when your budget is actually used as your guide to spending, and you find that it isn't working out as you had hoped, go back to negotiating with your new experience to help you make adjustments.

Remember, your spending should make Love Bank deposits in both of your Love Banks. If that's not happening, changes are in order.

## Consider This . . .

1. Create a budget that you both accept enthusiastically and that you are both willing to follow. If the wife has expressed a need for financial support, use the "Financial Support Inventory: Needs and Wants Budget" worksheets in the questionnaires section of the MarriageBuilders.com website, which can be copied without charge.

2. After creating a budget, do you and your spouse still have conflicts over financial management? Describe your conflicts as clearly as possible, and show respect for each other's opinions and perspective. Then, use the Policy of Joint Agreement and the Four Guidelines for Successful Negotiation to find a solution that accommodates the interests of both of you.

3. Do your financial decisions seem to make money a higher priority for you than your love for each other? How does the POJA always remind you to make each other your highest priority?

# 11

## Conflicts over Children

I began this book with an example of a typical marital conflict: Tony and Jodi couldn't agree on who would get up at night to calm Emily down when she started crying. Their failure to come to an enthusiastic agreement about that simple problem had a domino effect that almost led to their divorce.

If unresolved conflicts over everyday childcare responsibilities can lead to divorce, imagine what unresolved conflicts over child training and discipline can do to a marriage. Most parents know that the decisions they make about the moral and educational development of their children have a far greater effect on their ultimate happiness and success than decisions about who gets up with them at night. And when parents can't agree on the goals and methods of child training, it's bound to tear a couple apart.

If parents do not see eye to eye in the way children are to be raised, children become experts in using the "divide and conquer" strategy. You tell your son that he can't go out with his friends until he has made his bed and cleaned up his room. Then your spouse says that it's okay for him to go out this time, but he has to clean his room tomorrow. When one spouse tries to take control of raising children, and the other doesn't agree with those rules, the children learn very little about how to become successful in life. The lessons their parents try to teach them are judged to be anyone's guess because even the parents can't agree. So they go to their peers, other children, for advice—a notoriously poor source of wisdom.

But unilateral childrearing decisions do more than create confusion in children. They are also very offensive. Have you ever felt that your spouse has not supported you in the way you want to raise your children? It's a very common complaint in marriage and a huge source of Love Bank withdrawals. When parents don't agree on what a child should do, or how to punish a child for disobedience, a unilateral decision by one spouse is almost certain to make withdrawals in the other spouse's Love Bank. The one trying to protect the children often feels the pain of the discipline more acutely than the children do. But the one doing the disciplining can also be offended. He or she feels abandoned and unappreciated.

It's also a mistake to grant favors to children without mutual agreement. If one spouse gives something to a child that's not approved by the other spouse, the disapproving spouse can sometimes look like the evil parent who doesn't care enough about his or her children to give them what they really need. Unilateral giving of favors by a parent can sometimes cause as much resentment in marriage as unilateral discipline. It's unfair to characterize your spouse as unloving simply because you disagree about how to care for your children.

It's a mistake to reward or punish your children when your spouse does not agree with you with enthusiasm. If your spouse does not support your form of training, your children will not learn much from it. And you're sure to withdraw love units whenever that happens.

## Spouses with Blended Families Face a Particularly Difficult Challenge

My wife, Joyce, found small children to be very annoying when she was a teenager. She avoided babysitting. So when we married, I wasn't quite sure how she would handle our own children, or if she would even want to have any.

When our children did arrive, Joyce turned out to be a terrific mother. She was very patient with her own children—and grandchildren. But she still finds other people's children to be annoying.

That's part of the problem faced in blended families where at least one spouse has a child from a different relationship. It's tough enough to raise your own children, but your spouse's children can make the task seem impossible. The resentment that grows from a couple's failure to agree on childrearing decisions wrecks the vast majority of these marriages. Very few of them survive.

In blended families, independent childrearing decisions usually have a much greater negative effect on Love Bank balances than they do in nuclear families (where children are the offspring of both parents) because spouses have a natural instinct to protect their own at all costs. Any unilateral punishment by a stepparent is usually met with the natural parent's very angry defense of his or her child.

Each spouse in a blended family tends to put his or her own children's interests first. It's usually in an effort to compensate for the trauma their kids experienced at the death of a parent or a divorce. The guilt parents feel for having deprived their children of the advantages of a nuclear family often causes them to give them whatever they want. Discipline goes down the drain.

There's an additional problem that occurs when the original family's breakup was due to divorce rather than death—divorcing parents have set a very bad example for their children of how to behave. Rather than teaching their children by example to be considerate of others, one or both parents have proven to be so thoughtless that their love was destroyed, thus ending the marriage. As a result, their children learned that it's "every man for himself."

So if you're part of a blended family and you don't want your children interfering with your love for each other, and don't want to end up divorced, you should make all of your childrearing decisions with mutual and enthusiastic agreement. All disciplinary action and rewards should be decided before you implement them. Then your discipline will be taken seriously, neither of you will become the evil parent, and you'll be making Love Bank deposits instead of withdrawals.

## Men and Women Interpret the Goals of Raising Children Differently

What's a more important goal in raising children, obedience or knowing that they are loved? We'd all agree that they're both important, but if a decision must be made to achieve one and not the other, which would you choose?

In general, women tend to want their children to know that they are loved more than they want them to be obedient, and men tend to want them to be obedient more than they want them to feel loved.

How about learning to be self-reliant? Do you want your children to earn their allowance, or do you give it to them with no strings attached? Men tend to stress working for what you need, while women tend to want the need to be met one way or another.

While these differences do not describe every couple, they are only two of many common conflicts between men and women when raising children.

Who's right? Who's wrong? In most cases, parents' conflicting goals are both right. Children need to know they are loved and they should also be obedient. Children should learn to become self-reliant and their needs should be met. But how do you accomplish both?

What goals do each of you have when it comes to raising children? What are your priorities? Are they different? Do those differences lead to conflict when it comes to making decisions regarding how to discipline your children? The sooner you answer these questions and apply them to the way you resolve conflicts over childrearing, the better.

The perspective that each of you brings to childrearing is equally valuable. When you come to an enthusiastic agreement about the way you raise your children, they will benefit through your joint wisdom. On the other hand, if one of you makes a unilateral decision your children will be frustrated and confused. When one spouse disciplines a child without the other spouse's support, the child feels that one parent seems to love him more than the other. And when a child is rewarded by only one spouse he or she receives a mixed message. What he did was valuable from one parent's perspective, but not valuable from the other parent's perspective. Was it or wasn't it valuable? The child doesn't know for sure.

When you come to your children with a united front, with consistency, and with agreement, you deliver to your children a powerful message, lessons that are sure to impress them and point them in the right direction. Children clearly gain when both parents can agree on how they're to be raised. It eliminates confusion from mixed messages and stupid, emotional, and impulsive decisions made by one spouse in the heat of anger.

The failure to teach your children important lessons of life and the loss of your love for each other are the results if you cannot come to enthusiastic agreements about the way you raise your children. So I'm sure you agree with me that it's extremely important to become skilled in resolving such conflicts with a win-win outcome.

## How to Raise Your Children with Enthusiastic Agreement

Begin with a clear understanding of your goal: it's to follow the Policy of Joint Agreement. Don't tell your children what to do, punish them, reward them, or teach them until you have reached an enthusiastic agreement. Once an agreement is reached, you simply follow through. Further negotiation on that issue is unnecessary—it's settled.

So it would be a good first step to see where you agree and where you disagree regarding childrearing. I'm sure there have been recurring disagreements you can remember that can be written on a list titled "Conflicts." But you should also take some time making a list titled "No Conflicts." These are decisions that you have already made regarding childrearing that you both agree to enthusiastically. They can be made unilaterally without any risk of disagreement or offense. Over time, as you remember past incidents, and new challenges occur in your effort to train your children, you can add to both lists.

Once a situation is placed on the Conflicts list, any action related to it by either spouse is to await an agreement. In other words, neither of you may make a unilateral decision regarding that issue. If you can't agree to rewards or punishments regarding Johnny making his bed in the morning, you may not offer rewards or inflict punishment to encourage that objective until an enthusiastic agreement is reached.

After you have a list of conflicts to be resolved, the sooner you get to them, the better.

Remember that your negotiation must be safe and pleasant. Do not make any demands, be disrespectful, or become angry. If either of you find yourself becoming emotional, break off your conversation until you've had a chance to pull yourself together.

Describe the conflict clearly. Use a notebook that follows the form described in appendix A so that you both clearly understand the issue. Then, discover each other's opinions respectfully to understand what kind of a solution would work for both of you. Remember, there's wisdom in both of your perspectives.

After you have had a chance to understand each other, you're ready to brainstorm—think of solutions that might make both of you happy. Carry your notebook so you can jot down ideas as they come to you. Give your brain a chance to come up with some creative ideas.

Finally, try out one of your solutions that takes both of your perspectives into account. If it works well, you will both be enthusiastic about using it. It will have resolved your conflict.

## Consider This . . .

1. Have you been demanding, disrespectful, or angry when you've discussed childrearing issues with each other? Have you used any excuses for these abusive tactics to try to justify them?

2. Instead of arguing about how to raise your children, do you simply do what you think is right and hope that your spouse will adjust to it? What is the likely outcome when a spouse is expected to adjust to a decision that has not been enthusiastically accepted?

3. When does a childrearing decision become a Love Buster? Do either of you feel you have the right to make decisions about your children independently of the other's interests and feelings? Are you willing to give up that right by following the POJA for the sake of your love for each other?

4. Make two lists, one titled "Conflicts" that describes the conflicts you face over childrearing, and the other titled "No Conflicts" that describes issues that have been settled. Use the Policy of Joint Agreement and the Four Guidelines to Successful Negotiation to try to resolve each of the conflicts you have listed. Keep the notebook I recommend (see appendix A) close by to guide your discussion. Remember to use the "try it, you'll like it" test of a proposed remedy. And if the test doesn't create an enthusiastic agreement, go back to brainstorming.

5. For more insight into how to keep the pressures of childrearing from taking a toll on your marriage, read my book *His Needs, Her Needs for Parents: Keeping Romance Alive.*

# 12

## Conflicts over Sex

T he apostle Paul wrote concerning sex, "Do not deprive each other except perhaps by mutual consent" (1 Cor. 7:5). While the Policy of Joint Agreement that I've been recommending requires that you both enthusiastically agree before you have sex, Paul is saying that spouses should have sex unless they both agree not to do it. Later in the passage, knowing that the issue is complicated, he lets the reader know that it's a suggestion, not a command. His readers, especially women, heave a great sigh of relief when they come to that escape clause.

I fully understand Paul's dilemma. He knew that sex was very important in marriage and spouses should be encouraged to have a rich and fulfilling sexual relationship with each other. But trying to have sex on demand has its problems.

Frequent and fulfilling sex in marriage is as common a problem today as it was two thousand years ago. And as is the case with most ageless problems, the issue is definitely complicated. But from the perspective of many spouses, mostly men, it shouldn't be that way. What's complicated about a man and woman enjoying sex with each other?

At the time of marriage, most spouses, men and women both, consider frequent and fulfilling sex with each other to be one of the God-given benefits of marriage. But as time passes, men usually discover that their wives are not quite as interested in sex as they are. And the longer they're married the less interested their wives become. As sex becomes less and less frequent, husbands become more and more frustrated and disappointed. What had seemed almost effortless now becomes almost impossible. Men find that they don't know how to persuade their wives to get back to being the great lovers that they once were. With this issue, they lack negotiating skill.

If you find yourself in that position, and you simply can't seem to discuss the subject with your spouse, or your discussions get you nowhere, I'll show you how what you're learning in this book can be applied to conflicts over sex.

## Can You Discuss the Issue Safely and Cheerfully?

Sex is such an emotional need that calm and respectful discussion can be very difficult to achieve. I sometimes use an analogy of a thirsty man to illustrate a husband's frustration with his wife's sexual reluctance. It's as if he's unable to reach water while his wife can easily bring it to him if she's willing. She explains that she's too tired or not in the mood as he is becoming increasingly thirsty. But instead of negotiating with her, he makes demands: *Bring me some water right now!* When that doesn't work, he is disrespectful: *What a poor excuse for a wife you've turned out to be!* Then, as his frustration mounts, he loses his temper and starts to yell obscenities.

On the one hand, you can understand that the position he's in can be infuriating, but the methods he's using will not lead to her cooperation. They will drive her away. Instead of trying to help him, she'll avoid him. The same principle applies to getting the sex he needs. If he wants her to become a more fulfilling sex partner, he must make his discussion with her safe and pleasant.

The discussion itself should begin with a request for a change in how often or in the way you make love. After the request is on the table, you then each have an opportunity to explain your perspective on the issue to find a way to meet the request with mutual enthusiasm. Are there any differences that must be taken into account when trying to find an enthusiastic agreement?

I suggest that you begin your inquiry with a question. The answer to that question will help guide you toward a resolution to almost any conflict over sex. The question is: *Why should we have sex?*

## Why Should We Have Sex?

Men usually experience a craving for sex that builds over a few days, or for younger men over a few hours, after their last sexual release. Masturbation relieves that craving to some extent, but a sexual encounter with a woman is usually the most fulfilling. So for most men, their answer to the question "Why should we have sex?" is that sex is necessary to relieve their sexual craving. I call what most men do to gain that relief a "sexual act."

Women, on the other hand, don't usually experience the same sexual craving that men do. At least, it's not nearly as often. So for them, sex usually has a much different purpose. It's usually a small part of a larger whole that helps them create intimacy with the man they love. For most women, the answer to the question

"Why should we have sex?" is that sex is necessary for emotional bonding that builds on affection and intimate conversation. I call what most women do to achieve that objective a "sexual event."

Don't get me wrong. I'm not saying that husbands and wives consider the purpose of sex to be entirely one way or the other. There's usually a blend of motives as men also want sex for emotional bonding and women want relief for their sexual craving. But what I'm saying here is that the **primary** motives of husbands and wives to engage in sex with each other are usually very different.

The hormone testosterone helps explain why men view the purpose of sex as a release from a craving. This hormone, which is in abundance for most men and sadly (from the perspective of most men) in short supply for most women, creates their sexual craving. Women find that when they are administered the same amount of testosterone as is found in most nineteen-year-old men, they, too, tend to have a craving for sex, and find themselves searching for sexual relief as often as men.

As with men, there are probably physiological reasons for a woman's perspective regarding the necessity for sex. Hormones and neural pathways unique to women probably account for a woman's need for the intimacy that sex can provide. But whatever those physiological reasons are, they don't seem to motivate women to have sex as frequently as most men would like.

Procreation, of course, is the ultimate reason for sex. The physiology of both men and women unconsciously motivates them to have sex with each other to perpetuate their species. Sometimes that purpose can be conscious, and they deliberately engage in sex to have a child. But that is not the usual reason that husbands and wives give for having sex. And those reasons motivate them to have sex even when they have no ability or desire to procreate.

## How Should We Have Sex?

In your effort to respectfully gather relevant information on each other's perspective regarding sex, the next question you should discuss is "How should we have sex?" The answer to that question depends mightily on the answer to the first question, "Why should we have sex?"

If left to their own devices, most men would choose a method of sex that reflects their purpose, which is to satisfy a craving that they experience far more intensely and far more often than their wives. They would initiate a sex act by doing what it takes to create sexual arousal for themselves. For most men, looking at and feeling their wife's body, especially breasts, buttocks, and crotch, usually works best. The most convenient time for this sex act is while their wives are in bed with them before going to sleep or upon awakening. The sex act itself usually involves intercourse, but many men prefer oral sex because they find it to be quicker and more intense.

Again, don't get me wrong. I'm not suggesting that all husbands behave this way or even think this way. I'm merely saying that without any resistance or direction from their wives, it makes sense for most men to have marital sex frequently and in the most stimulating way possible. So in your discussion, be completely honest about your instincts. Tell your wife what would please you the most if she were not to object.

Based on a wife's perspective that sex should be a bonding experience that builds on affection and intimate conversation, she would have a much different answer to the question "How should we have sex?" She would want sex to be part of a much larger romantic experience. Dining, dancing, and moonlit walks, all generously infused with expressions of care, are examples of the foreplay that would lead her to a fulfilling sexual experience. Technically, if he does just about anything to demonstrate his care for her, like washing and drying the dishes after dinner so she can take it easy for a while, she might be willing to make love. But since all women are different, and I certainly can't speak for you, give your husband an honest answer that would reflect your most preferred way to make love to him.

By the time you reach this stage of negotiation with each other, your differing perspectives on how you should have sex with each other will help you understand why you've been having conflicts over sex. I think you will be able to demonstrate my point that sex is usually a singular "act" for the husband and usually a much larger "event" for the wife.

With such a wide difference in perspective, how can a husband and wife be expected to reach an enthusiastic agreement regarding how and how often they will make love? Having sex his way makes her feel like a receptacle—something he uses to merely relieve his sexual craving. Having sex her way makes him feel that she is imposing conditions that make the frequent sex he needs essentially impossible for him.

At the risk of being annoyingly redundant, bear in mind that I know that both husbands and wives look for sexual release and intimacy when they make love. In fact, there are some men who crave intimacy more than their wives, and some wives who crave sexual release more than their husbands. But I think it's useful to know that there is usually a significant difference between husbands and wives regarding the primary purpose of sex, and how sex should be expressed. Once that difference is understood, you're in a position to find a way to increase sexual frequency with mutual enthusiastic agreement.

## How to Make Love More Often and More Passionately

After you have each other's answers to questions of why and how you and your spouse should have sex, you're ready to brainstorm resolutions to the issue that's been raised. Assuming the issue has something to do with increasing sexual frequency and/or improving sexual satisfaction, I generally recommend that a couple think of ways that they can turn sexual acts into sexual events.

In my book *His Needs, Her Needs*, I begin my chapter on affection with the observation that when a man creates an environment of affection (affection throughout the day), he creates the conditions that make sex an event for her. Intimate conversation is also included in this observation. If his ongoing affection and conversation help her feel bonded to him emotionally, sex adds an important dimension to her feeling of intimacy.

An assignment that I have often given couples who struggle with the issue of sexual frequency is for them to engage in three hours of affection and intimate conversation before having sex. Most men who have not learned to create an environment of affection for their wives feel at first that it's too much work just to have sex because they're not in the habit of meeting her emotional needs. But after they practice doing it for a while and get the hang of it, they find themselves being affectionate and conversant almost effortlessly. It turns out not to be work at all. Instead of thinking of it as a requirement for sex, they consider it to be essential to their relationship.

When a husband meets his wife's needs for affection and intimate conversation, she finds it much easier to meet his need for sexual fulfillment. Of course, the converse is also true. The more she meets his need for sexual fulfillment, the easier it is for him to meet her emotional needs for affection and intimate conversation.

I've written a rule for couples that helps them make massive Love Bank deposits. It also helps them turn sexual acts into sexual events. I call it the Policy of Undivided Attention: *Give your spouse your undivided attention a minimum of fifteen hours each week, using the time to meet each other's emotional needs for affection, intimate conversation, sexual fulfillment, and recreational companionship.* Couples who follow this rule are able to increase their frequency of lovemaking with enthusiastic agreement because sex becomes fulfilling for both husband and wife. They usually plan a four-hour date four times a week where all four emotional needs are met on each date. You'll find more information on how to be mutually enthusiastic about the way you make love in my book *His Needs, Her Needs* (chapter 4—Sexual Fulfillment).

## Special Problems with Sex

Making love to someone for whom you care deeply and who cares deeply for you is one of life's most enjoyable and fulfilling experiences. But many spouses, especially wives, find that what should be enjoyable turns into a nightmare. In the beginning of their marriage, a husband's perspective on sex overrules her perspective, and so he forces her to have sex with him on his terms. Complying with his demands, she associates sex with a demeaning and sometimes painful experience. Instead of a way to express his love for her, sex becomes one of his most selfish acts. Eventually, it becomes the last thing she wants to do with her husband. She has developed an aversion to sex.

In those cases, I help a wife overcome her sexual aversion before encouraging her to have sex with her husband. In my Q&A

column, "How to Overcome Sexual Aversion," at the Marriage Builders.com website, I describe the method I use to help a wife overcome an aversion to sex. It involves associating sex with love and comfort instead of selfishness and fear. After the aversion is overcome, her husband learns to make love to her in a way that expresses his care for her, rather than only his craving. Affection and intimate conversation usually provide the environment, followed by a personally satisfying sequence of touching that helps trigger sexual arousal for her. She also discovers positions and movements that create the most intense pleasure for her. After her husband learns how to make love to her in a way that is sexually and emotionally enjoyable for her, she is in a position to negotiate with him about having sex more often.

A related problem some women experience is pain during intercourse caused by vaginismus, a muscle spasm that closes the opening to the vagina. A yeast infection is usually the original culprit, but there are a host of other possible causes as well. The trick to overcoming this condition is to gently stimulate the vaginal opening without triggering the reflex. Daily exercises that slowly introduce ever-larger amply lubricated objects to the opening usually solve the problem within a few weeks. I offer a more detailed description of this recommended method in my article "How to Overcome Pain during Intercourse" in the Q&A section of the MarriageBuilders.com website.

If you try to have intercourse with pain, it will only make matters worse. It strengthens the painful muscle reflex until it becomes impossible to tolerate. On the other hand, even if you experience vaginismus occasionally, when your lovemaking always follows the Policy of Joint Agreement you will be able to overcome it the right way. Thoughtfulness is the solution to most marital problems.

Yet another problem faced by couples trying to resolve sexual conflicts is their tendency to fight. A point often made by wives is that the time taken for affection and conversation can be ruined by an argument. It's the opposite of affection and intimate conversation. While that sounds logical to most women, men often don't seem to get it. They expect their wives to be sexually receptive regardless of what went on before, because they would feel that way. An argument doesn't necessarily lower a man's sex drive, but it certainly creates enough emotional distance for a woman to crush her desire for a bonding experience. I've been writing for years that arguing in marriage should be avoided at all costs. But that's especially true if you want to make love more often.

Every marriage is unique, so some of what I've written may not apply to you. Sometimes it's the wife who wants to make love more often. In this case a husband may have lost his craving for sex due to lower testosterone levels. The solution to that problem is to see his physician for a testosterone supplement. Or it may be that his wife has made sex so unpleasant for him that he has developed an aversion. The recommendation I make for wives with an aversion to sex also works for husbands.

Sexual inexperience can also create sexual conflicts in marriage. For a couple, or even just one spouse, to enter marriage without knowing how to have a sexual experience complete with all five stages (willingness, arousal, plateau, climax, and recovery) can create a honeymoon disaster. The worksheets in *Five Steps to Romantic Love* can help a couple gain the experience they need to fully understand their own and each other's sexual responses. It's an understanding that's absolutely necessary for marriage.

When I suggested sexual training to a couple recently, the wife responded by saying that she didn't want to be part of a "science experiment." She felt that if a couple were right for each other, they shouldn't have to learn to enjoy sex with each other—it should just happen naturally. In one sense, she has a point. A couple in love finds that their sexual responsiveness toward each other is so greatly enhanced that they don't have to do much to trigger every stage of the sexual experience. But when one or both spouses loses that feeling of love, understanding their sexual response so that they can create it with each other almost at will gives them a great advantage in being able to restore their love. Having a fulfilling sexual experience with each other is one of the best ways to make massive Love Bank deposits.

I want you to have what you need in your marriage. And I'm sure that you want to give each other what you need. The only thing standing in your way is failure to understand and respect each other's perspective whenever a conflict arises. The recognition that your perspectives complement each other—they both contain some truth that should be addressed in a final enthusiastic resolution—helps you see solutions that go beyond what either of you would have found on your own. Together you make wiser choices and meet each other's needs in a much more fulfilling way. You'll find that when you make love in a way that addresses both of your reasons for having sex, you will be completely fulfilled by it.

## Consider This . . .

1. Have you been demanding, disrespectful, or angry when you've discussed issues about sex with each other? Have you used any excuses for these abusive tactics to try to justify them?

2. Instead of arguing about sex, do you simply do what you please and hope that your spouse will adjust to it? What is the likely outcome when a spouse is expected to adjust to a decision that has not been enthusiastically accepted? Discuss with each other how unilateral decisions about any sex acts outside of your marriage affect each other (such as pornography, masturbation, etc.).

3. When does a decision regarding sex become a Love Buster? Do either of you feel you have the right to make decisions about sex independently of the other's interests and feelings? Are you willing to give up that right by following the POJA for the sake of your love for each other?

4. Describe conflicts you have over sex as clearly as possible and respectfully learn each other's perspectives. Use the Policy of Joint Agreement and the Four Guidelines to Successful Negotiation to try to resolve these conflicts by creating a solution that you both accept enthusiastically and are both willing to follow. You may find the worksheets in the workbook *Five Steps to Romantic Love* helpful in guiding you through the creation and implementation of your solution. The worksheets also support chapter 4 (Sexual Fulfillment) in *His Needs, Her Needs*.

# PART 3

# Common Problems
# with Marital Conflict Resolution

L et's say you know the rules, and you are trying to follow the procedure I've recommended. But you are still finding the resolution to certain conflicts elusive. If so, this section will address some of the common barriers couples face in finding win-win solutions to their problems, and how to overcome them.

# 13

## How to Negotiate
## When You Are Emotional

You've tried to avoid fighting because you know that it doesn't really solve anything. But you get so upset by the way your spouse treats you, or ignores you, that you can't help yourself. And when you try discussing problems with your spouse, you get even more upset by the way he or she reacts.

Does that describe your situation?

It's a vicious cycle. The problems you face in your marriage upset you terribly. They must be solved now. You've tried to communicate their urgency, but your spouse isn't cooperating. So you break the cardinal rule of negotiating by being demanding, disrespectful, and angry. That gets your spouse's attention, but instead of seeing the urgency of your problems, your spouse comes to believe that nothing you discuss can be resolved rationally. So instead of even attempting to solve your problems, your spouse ignores them, which upsets you terribly.

The primary advantage to being emotional in marriage is that conflicts keep getting addressed even if it means having nasty fights. But the disadvantage is that the conflicts are rarely *resolved*. And the way an emotional person tends to go about trying to get his or her spouse's attention makes massive Love Bank withdrawals. The conflicts remain while their love for each other is slipping away. So how can an emotional person ever hope to have a marriage that works? How can such a person be happily married when they can't seem to resolve any of their conflicts?

Well, I have good news. Emotional people *can* resolve their marital conflicts. I've witnessed their success in thousands of marriages. But the solution begins with the realization that they can learn to discuss their problems calmly and rationally. Regardless of how emotional you have been in the past, you can learn to approach life's problems with grace and wisdom.

Begin your quest to become a calm and wise negotiator with the assumption that win-win resolutions to marital conflicts can be found only when spouses discuss their problems calmly and rationally, looking for solutions that make both spouses happy. Any attempt to be demanding, disrespectful, or angry will prevent you from resolving your conflict, and it will destroy your love for each other.

Next, assume that only you can control your emotional reactions—no one else can do it for you. And you can learn to do it.

Granted, your spouse can be frustrating. He or she can fail to provide what you need in life, and can say and do things that make you very unhappy. But the way you respond is up to you. No one forces you to make demands, show disrespect, or have angry outbursts.

Let's stop here to think this through for a moment. If you don't agree with these two assumptions, you're not ready for my plan. Unless you realize that your problems will be solved only if you discuss them calmly with a win-win goal in mind, and take full responsibility for your emotional reactions, not blaming them on your spouse, you will not be able to develop the right frame of mind to tackle the conflicts that are common in marriage.

But if you accept these assumptions, your first step toward becoming an expert marital problem-solver will be to learn to be calm in the midst of frustration.

## Train Yourself to Relax

An angry outburst is only one of many emotional reactions to frustration, and I've not only helped train others to completely eliminate them, but I've also learned how to eliminate them myself. When I was young, I had a very bad temper, as did most of the other members of my family. But when I came to realize that my anger was self-defeating, and that no one made me lose my temper, I set out to eliminate my outbursts completely. In spite of some very frustrating experiences I've had in life, I have not lost my temper in over fifty years.

The procedure I recommend to overcome angry outbursts is very similar to the way most emotional reactions can be overcome. It begins with the realization that no one makes you react emotionally. Whether it's an angry outburst or any other intense emotional reaction, it's yours and you are completely responsible for it. Your spouse can't control your emotional reactions. Only you can control them.

Most intense emotional reactions are neurologically similar. An angry outburst and a panic attack have many of the same features—and the way to overcome them is essentially the same.

When faced with a threat, we either fight or flee. Either we stand up to the threat and defeat it, or we run for cover. If you fight, you'll have an angry reaction, and if you flee, you'll have an anxiety reaction. But in either case, it's the adrenaline in your system that magnifies your reaction.

So the best way to control an angry outburst or a panic attack is to reduce the adrenaline in your bloodstream. While there are many dietary and medical ways to help achieve that objective, or prevent it from happening in the first place, one of the simplest approaches to controlling your emotional reactions is to learn to relax, and to be able to do so almost instantly. Effective relaxation techniques can be learned within a few days if they are practiced often enough. And if they are practiced while thinking about some of your most frustrating situations, you prepare yourself for effective negotiation.

Just as you might prepare for a marathon by training your body to run ever-longer distances, you can train your brain to approach frustrating situations with intelligence rather than emotion. Every frustrating situation you find yourself in is a training opportunity. By relaxing instead of attacking (or fleeing), you create an opportunity to approach the situation with thoughtfulness.

While most of us know if we're tense or relaxed, some people find it helpful to use some form of biofeedback to help them quantify their efforts. A simple galvanic response meter can do the trick, and they can be purchased online for between fifty and one hundred dollars. An audio CD that teaches relaxation techniques often accompanies the meter.*

The purpose of relaxation training using a biofeedback meter is to learn to relax under conditions of high stress. At first, you simply learn to raise and lower the meter reading by changing your thoughts. Think of an unpleasant stressful situation, and the reading

---

*The GSR2 Biofeedback Relaxation System with CD by Bio-Medical Instruments, Inc. costs about $75.

rises; think of a pleasant non-stressful situation, and the reading lowers. After you can manipulate the meter by simply thinking stressful and non-stressful thoughts, your next challenge is to keep the reading low even when thinking about a stressful situation. You do that by deliberately relaxing every muscle in your body, thereby flushing out all of the adrenaline. With practice, your relaxation can be demonstrated on the biofeedback meter in a matter of seconds.

When you have mastered relaxation while alone, the next challenge is to keep the biofeedback reading low when you discuss a problem with your spouse. At first, you may think that all of your training doesn't amount to much when applied to real-life situations. But with some practice, you will be just as successful with your spouse present as you were alone.

By keeping the meter reading low, you are controlling your emotional reactions, giving your brain a chance to think of real solutions to your problems. But when you become emotional, your creative ability is seriously downgraded, leaving you with few ideas that are worth considering.

If both you and your spouse can guarantee that your discussion will not lead to an emotional outburst, you will not only be far more creative and successful in finding solutions, but you will be more likely to raise problems with each other. Joyce and I tackle conflicts as they arise, and at least one will arise just about every hour we're together. Obviously, if we did not handle our conflicts the right way, our lives would be filled with arguments—or we would not be dealing with them at all.

By controlling our emotional reactions, Joyce and I follow the first guideline for successful negotiation in marriage: to make the discussion safe and enjoyable. You are to avoid making any demands, avoid showing any disrespect, and avoid becoming angry. In other words, you're to avoid becoming emotional.

If you can't control your emotional reaction, you can't follow the second guideline: to understand the conflict and its possible resolutions from each other's perspectives with profound respect for each other—something terribly missing when spouses become emotional.

The third guideline, to brainstorm solutions with the goal of making both spouses happy with the outcome, is impossible to follow without the second guideline in place. And finally, the fourth guideline, to select a resolution that makes both spouses happy, can't be followed if the third guideline isn't followed.

So it all comes down to knowing how to control your emotional reactions. If you can learn how to relax, keeping your emotional reactions at bay while discussing marital conflict, you'll have a much easier time resolving your conflicts. But if you can't control them, your problems will remain unsolved. It's that simple.

# 14

## How to Negotiate
## When No One Wants
## to Raise the Issue

Are there problems in your marriage that have been festering for years? Have you lost hope of ever resolving them because they are never discussed? Are you afraid to bring them up?

Successful negotiation in marriage is a skill that should be taught in school along with reading, writing, and arithmetic. That's because successful marital negotiation leads to happy marriages, and that, in turn, creates productive families that make our entire culture flourish.

But sadly, most couples are not skilled in marital negotiation. When a conflict arises, they either fight over it or sweep it under the rug.

Suppose that you and your spouse want to take a vacation, but can't agree on where to go. One of you wants to spend a week at a campground four miles from your home, while the other would prefer a week in Orlando, visiting Disney World, SeaWorld, and Universal Studios. Your children have all voted for the Orlando trip. You don't want to fight about it, but haven't learned how to negotiate. By avoiding the subject, no vacation at all looms on the horizon.

So to go on any vacation, one of you decides to capitulate. You either go camping or visit Orlando, depending on who does the capitulating. I've called that the sacrifice strategy for resolving marital problems. That's one way to solve a problem without having to discuss it. But the capitulator ends up feeling very resentful. The one wanting a Florida vacation will be very unhappy camping, especially if it rains, and the one wanting to camp will not be cheered up by Mickey.

Sexual conflicts are often handled the same way. One of you wants sex more often than the other, so one person sacrifices, either agreeing to more sex than they want or putting up with less sex than they want. Either way, the problem is not discussed and resentment is the final result.

Of course, there's always the option of no vacation, where neither are willing to budge—or negotiate. And the issue of how often to have sex can turn into not having sex at all when spouses won't talk about the issue with each other. Resentment builds to such an extent that the capitulator finally decides not to capitulate any longer. Nothing happens. Not even a fight.

Does this describe the way you deal with conflicts? You pretend as if they don't exist? If you have piles of unspoken issues in your marriage, I want to encourage you to get them out on the table this week and start negotiating. Here's one way to do it.

## Write a Letter

The problem with talking about conflicts that have been buried for years is that when they are raised, they tend to explode in your face. So much emotion has been festering that when the topic is introduced, demands, disrespect, and anger often destroy any hope of a thoughtful and intelligent resolution.

Remember, the first guideline for successful negotiation in marriage is to make the discussion safe and pleasant. If you try to talk about the problem, you may find that your emotions get the best of you and you simply can't proceed. But if you negotiate in writing, even if you are seething while you describe your problem, you can edit your initial emotionally charged words and rewrite any sentences that would be interpreted by your spouse as demanding, disrespectful, or angry.

Your letter should begin with an explanation for why you are putting your problem in writing rather than talking about it. It might look something like this:

> *Hi Honey,*
>
> *I know that this may seem to be a strange way for me to introduce a problem to you, but I'm afraid that I might have trouble making myself clear if we were to talk about it. So if you would indulge me, I'd like to introduce something that has been bothering me so that we can work together toward a solution. This is a problem that we have had for some time now, but I think we have both avoided dealing with it for a variety of reasons. Maybe by writing to each other about it, we can come to a resolution.*

The next section of the letter should state the conflict and offer your perspective on how it might be resolved. Again, remember to avoid writing anything that sounds demanding, disrespectful, or angry.

> *The problem I'd like us to solve is that, from my perspective, we are not making love often enough, and when we do it's not in ways that satisfy me. I would like to make love at least twice a week, and before we make love, I'd like us to spend some time talking to each other and being affectionate. I think that we could do this if we scheduled time to be together each week for that purpose—like having a date.*

After you've stated the problem and described your perspective, you should ask for your spouse's perspective. How does he or she feel about the problem itself and about your proposed solution?

> *How do you feel about it? Do you also feel that we're not making love often enough, and that we're not doing it in ways that satisfy you? If so, how would you like to solve this problem? Or, if you are happy with how often we make love and find that the way we do it is fulfilling to you, would you help me with this problem I've been having? What would you suggest to satisfy my need? Please write me a response so that we can begin solving this problem together.*

I know that this letter sounds very formal and somewhat awkward. But my point is that this is one way to bring up a problem that has been buried too long.

Once the problem is on the table, your spouse will either respond to it or ignore it. Let's first consider ways that your spouse might respond.

1. **A proactive response.** Your spouse responds in writing with empathy and creativity. He or she apologizes for failing to

meet this very important need and expresses a willingness to try just about anything to resolve it. He or she suggests that you plan two dates a week that will begin by being alone with each other to talk and be affectionate, just like you did before you were married. Then at the end of that time together you would make love. You would discuss by letter your reactions to each of your "dates" so that you could improve upon them. If either of you feels that changes would be helpful, you would write each other about it without making demands, being disrespectful, or becoming angry. When you feel safe, you could start discussing it face-to-face.

2. **A defensive response.** You receive a letter in a timely manner, but it begins by blaming you for the problem. If you would not be so busy, or if you would be a better lover, or if you would not be so moody, etc., etc., you would not have this problem. While those issues could be discussed respectfully, your spouse turns them into disrespectful accusations. This kind of reaction is the primary reason that you have not solved the problem earlier. You need help in knowing how to negotiate. Your next letter might suggest that you read together the first five chapters of my book *Love Busters*, which teaches couples how to avoid demands, disrespect, and anger. Then, when educated in how to negotiate safely, you proceed to solve your problems proactively.

3. **No response.** Occasionally, when one of my clients writes this letter to get the ball rolling, their spouse rips it up and throws it away. Or they don't even acknowledge receiving the letter. In cases like these, I usually recommend planning for a separation, while at the same time sending the letter again, using slightly different words, mentioning the fact that your

problem needs to be addressed. A spouse who is unwilling to respond to repeated communications of a problem is emotionally divorced. He or she has violated the vow to care for their spouse, which is the purpose of marriage itself. If two years of separation go by without the other spouse becoming willing to solve problems respectfully and intelligently, the neglected spouse usually comes to the conclusion that he or she no longer has a partner in marriage and files for divorce. Sometimes that jogs the other spouse into action, but even if the divorce goes through, the fact that the other spouse was no longer willing to provide necessary marital care means that the marriage was over years earlier. But in most cases, I've found that couples learn to discuss their problems effectively while separated, and then live together fulfilled.

I've counseled many retired couples who finally address problems they've endured through most of their marriage. They're happy that they were finally able to solve them, but wish that it had been done much earlier in their marriage. The busyness of raising children and developing careers distracted them enough to keep their problems unresolved.

Don't sweep your marital conflicts under the rug. If you've been afraid to raise issues in your marriage, try using the letter I've recommended. Make conflicts that have been bothering you a top priority in your life. And, with respect for each other, resolve them.

# 15

## How to Negotiate
## When You Are Indecisive

A common objection to the Policy of Joint Agreement is that it leaves one spouse languishing in limbo while the other is carefully considering all options. That's because the default condition for the POJA is to do nothing until you reach an enthusiastic agreement. And for most conflicts, doing nothing puts the couple in a lose-lose predicament.

I've found that, with practice, any couple can learn to come to an enthusiastic agreement when faced with a conflict. But I will admit that it takes more practice when one spouse is indecisive.

On average, women tend to be more indecisive than men. Considering the abundance of neural connections in the female brain that we discussed earlier, this should be no surprise—women have more information to process. And there's another factor that contributes to this inclination—women tend to be somewhat more anxious than men. Tests that measure emotional reactions, such as the Minnesota Multiphasic Personality Inventory (Hathaway and McKinley), adjust their scales to compensate for the measurable differences in anxiety between men and women. A score that would be judged abnormally anxious for men is considered to be normal for women, evidence that women tend to be more anxious than men.

But anxiety, and its resulting indecisiveness, should not be viewed as a personality flaw. While it might frustrate someone with a more impulsive way of making a decision, in the grand scope of things indecisiveness can often prevent a couple from making rash choices.

When a husband and wife respect each other's decision-making style, whether it's impulsive or indecisive, and continue to negotiate until an enthusiastic agreement is reached, they can benefit from the best of both styles and avoid the worst of them. Clearly, impulsive decision-making can get a person into quite a bit of trouble. But if indecisiveness leaves someone paralyzed, that can't be good, either. By encouraging an impulsive person to take more time to consider other options, and encouraging an indecisive person to test options to see how they work, both people benefit.

Have you ever had a conflict over choosing a color for a room in your house? An impulsive person can make the decision and have the drop cloths and paint brushes ready for action in no time. An indecisive person, on the other hand, may strain over thousands of color chips, wondering how changes in lighting will affect each color throughout the day. Does one of you tend to make snap decisions while the other waits to consider all of the options? How can such a couple ever come to an enthusiastic agreement?

If you practice using the Four Guidelines to Successful Negotiation, you will come to realize that both impulsiveness and indecisiveness can be accommodated. You will learn to avoid impulsive decisions by considering each other's perspectives carefully. Yet you will also avoid indecisiveness by making at least tentative decisions in a timely manner. You will learn to test a possible resolution to a conflict before a final agreement. You learn these important lessons as you come to understand and appreciate each other.

And there is one very important caveat to remember. If the test of a resolution turns out to be not as mutually enjoyable as expected, go back to brainstorming. If you choose a color for the room and it doesn't have the effect that one spouse thought it would have, paint the room a different color. Knowing that a bad decision can be corrected makes it easier for an indecisive person to take risks.

By using the guidelines, impulsive people learn the wisdom of taking more time to make a decision, and indecisive people learn that testing a possibility doesn't lead to disaster if it doesn't work out as well as expected. Very few decisions in life have to be set in cement. Almost all of them can be modified to make a couple's life more mutually enjoyable.

The time you take to make a tentative decision when you have a conflict should be discussed when you introduce the issue. And time should be set aside to discuss the possibilities. There is comfort in knowing that the conflict is at least being addressed, and when a tentative date for a test of possible resolutions is set, your creative juices can fly.

When you make a decision that is accepted with mutual enthusiasm, it will usually stay in place for quite some time. That's because it's a lifestyle decision that makes both of you happy. So you will not find yourselves returning to the same conflicts if they are resolved the right way. Granted, if one of you tends to be indecisive, the decision itself may take longer to make, but once it's made with mutual enthusiasm, it solves the problem and maintains your love for each other.

# 16

## How to Negotiate When Doing Nothing Is What One Spouse Wants

The default condition for the Policy of Joint Agreement is to do nothing. When you are in conflict over what to do, and have not yet found a win-win resolution, you are to do nothing until an enthusiastic agreement is reached.

Sometimes a couple is confused over what "do nothing" means. Do you continue to do what you've been doing or do you stop doing it? For example, if Joyce feels that the speed I'm driving makes her nervous, and she would like me to slow down, do I continue driving at my current speed until we have arrived at an enthusiastic agreement? After all, if I were to slow to the speed that makes her comfortable, I would be doing what she wants to do—a losing outcome for me. In this example, doing nothing means pulling off to the side of the road and discussing the conflict until an enthusiastic agreement is reached.

Obviously, the default condition is not the solution to a conflict. In fact, it's often worse than continuing to do whatever it is that bothers the other spouse. Its purpose is not to settle the issue, but rather to force a couple to take the time to solve it the right way once and for all.

But what if doing nothing is precisely what your spouse wants as a final outcome? It's win-lose by default.

This problem often appears when financial decisions are to be made. The husband wants to buy new fishing gear, and the wife is opposed to the purchase. Application of the default condition of the Policy of Joint Agreement rules out the purchase, so the wife wins and the husband loses. The wife wants to buy new backpacks for the children, but the husband feels that last year's model is still adequate. No backpacks this year. The husband wins and the wife loses.

To avoid that very unsatisfactory dilemma, I encourage spouses to put all unresolved conflicts on the front burner until an enthusiastic agreement can be found for them. In other words, doing nothing should not be an outcome tolerated by either spouse.

## Skill and Goodwill Help Keep Negotiation Alive

The primary reason that couples avoid discussing conflicts in marriage is that it usually doesn't turn out well. The discussion usually ends up in a fight. But if you have been practicing the Four Guidelines for Successful Negotiation, you are learning how to make these discussions pleasant and safe. You are also finding it easier to resolve conflicts with mutual enthusiasm. That makes it easier to mention them as they occur.

Some very highly emotionally charged conflicts may still be out of reach for you, but as you continue to practice resolving lesser issues, your skill will develop to a point where you can handle anything.

But besides building negotiating skill, you may have already noticed something else happening: you are building goodwill toward each other. That's because negotiating skill requires you to develop a better understanding of each other so that you can both be satisfied with the outcome. You're learning how to watch each other's back.

The mark of a good negotiator is goodwill toward the negotiating partner. One of the main reasons that Joyce and I handle conflicts so well is that we want to find resolutions that make both of us happy. We cannot rest if we know that one of us is unhappy with the status quo. If doing nothing makes one of us unhappy, we make time to work together to straighten out the problem. That's how effective negotiators feel toward each other.

If you become effective negotiators, you will have developed goodwill toward each other. You will not find yourselves willing to settle for a "do nothing" outcome. You will keep the issue alive until a solution is found.

So if one of you is willing to settle for the default condition of the POJA, knowing that the other is unhappy with that outcome, you have not practiced negotiating long enough to become effective negotiators. You should continue to practice coming to an enthusiastic agreement with minor conflicts, learning how to find win-win instead of win-lose resolutions. As you become more skilled, your goodwill toward each other will develop, making you less likely to accept a status quo that makes one of you unhappy.

As with all marital conflicts that are not resolved within a reasonable period of time, when a couple gets stuck, it's sometimes helpful to get creative ideas from other sources. One possibility is to consult with an expert in finding solutions to specific marital problems. I am asked almost daily to help couples think of a resolution to their conflict that they might both agree to enthusiastically. My answer is usually accompanied by a rationale designed to convince both spouses that it's the right path to follow.

But another valuable source of creative solutions is the Marriage Builders Forum found at the MarriageBuilders.com website. Thousands of people have joined this community to help couples find win-win resolutions to their conflicts, and it's entirely free of charge. Many of these people have become experts at resolving all sorts of marital conflicts.

The more you come to understand the value of finding win-win solutions to marital problems, and the more skilled you become in finding them, the closer you will feel toward each other. With both of you wanting happiness for each other, you will reject permanent outcomes that leave either of you dissatisfied, including the "do nothing" default condition of the Policy of Joint Agreement.

# 17

## How to Negotiate
## When You're Not Enthusiastic
## about Much

A s a clinical psychologist, I have been trained to help people who are suffering from depression. These are people who experience very little joy in life, and plenty of sorrow. They have great difficulty finding anything to be enthusiastic about. Does that describe the way you or your spouse feels? If so, would that rule you out of marital negotiation?

My requirement of "enthusiastic" agreement in marriage is, in part, to discourage "reluctant" agreement. I don't want couples to settle for lifestyle choices in which one spouse feels pressured or obligated to agree. When that happens, even though there is agreement, it's not actually a win-win outcome. I want couples to hold out for choices that will give them mutual happiness. Those are the choices that make the most Love Bank deposits. Win-win decisions help a couple stay in love.

But they do something else that clinical psychologists have observed: they keep people from being depressed. The more decisions a person makes that are clearly in their own interest, the happier they tend to be (as long as they are not at the expense of others). When they make reluctant decisions, they tend to be depressed.

So I've witnessed a pattern when it comes to marital negotiation. When reluctant agreement is accepted as an outcome, at least one spouse often ends up feeling depressed, incapable of being enthusiastic about much. And when a spouse is depressed, reluctant agreement seems to be their only option since they don't feel enthusiastic about anything very often.

How should a couple go about breaking that pattern?

Before I answer that question, let me offer you a short clinical course on depression.

I'll begin with a definition: depression is the feeling of sadness usually due to a sense of irretrievable loss. A depressed person feels incapable of ever being happy because they've lost what would have given them fulfillment. Happiness seems unattainable to them without it.

Some examples of depression due to irretrievable loss are reasonable. The death of a loved one is a common example. Health problems that are expected to lead to a painful death are another. An example in the realm of marriage is depression due to an affair. Even if the unfaithful spouse ends the affair and wants to restore the marriage, the betrayed spouse often feels that their loss of trust in the unfaithful spouse is irretrievable. And without trust they can never be happily married again.

And yet, even in cases where a loss is catastrophic, most people find happiness in something else. In other words, depression is

150

rarely permanent. People often overcome their feeling of depression and go on to be happy.

There is an element of truth *and* an element of irrationality in people who are depressed. It's true that they may have lost something that gave them happiness, but it's not true that they cannot be happy again without it. And that brings us to my next point: the two types of depression—endogenous and situational. *Endogenous* depression has a physiological cause with little or no clear rational basis. There doesn't appear to be any real loss. *Situational* depression, on the other hand, is due primarily to lifestyle factors, where the loss is quite apparent.

Almost all of the cases of depression I've treated during my career have been primarily situational. When I discover the lifestyle conditions that cause depression, and help change those conditions to my client's advantage, the depression usually disappears.

But I am also aware of the physiology of depression—the endogenous factor. A loss tends to trigger neurophysiological events that make matters worse. They create the feeling of depression that makes a person feel helpless to find solutions to their problems. So I usually recommend that a depressed person take antidepressant medication to counter these unproductive neurophysiological reactions. That helps them feel more optimistic about changes they need to make in their lifestyle, and it helps them make those changes.

Without antidepressant medication, people who tend to be depressed also tend to make reluctant decisions that help sustain their depressing lifestyle. No sooner do I help them remove an unpleasant lifestyle condition and replace it with something better than they make a decision that causes some new unpleasant condition to enter their life. The solution to their problem is to avoid making reluctant decisions altogether, and try to make as many enthusiastic decisions as possible. But while depressed, they don't believe that those alternatives exist.

As I mentioned, it's a pattern that is very self-defeating. If you don't believe that you can be enthusiastic about anything, you'll tend to settle for reluctant agreements that will tend to make you depressed. If you're depressed you believe that you can't be enthusiastic about anything.

## What Now?

So how does this analysis apply to the question: How should a couple negotiate when at least one spouse is not enthusiastic about much?

First, if you're not enthusiastic about much, it's very likely that you're clinically depressed. Depression is the most common mental disorder, and treatment for depression is usually very successful. So you should be evaluated by a clinical psychologist or psychiatrist who specializes in treating depression. If the therapist is qualified, he or she will encourage you to take an antidepressant medication to help you feel more optimistic about making positive changes in your lifestyle. Then the therapist will work with you to help make those changes. When the changes are in place, you will no longer need to take the medicine because your depression will have lifted.

Second, after you have overcome depression, you should try to make all new lifestyle decisions using the POJA. Since you will be more optimistic about finding win-win resolutions to the conflicts you face in your marriage, and you will be more creative as a result, you will be successful.

Consider for a moment how your depression has been affecting your Love Bank. Since it causes you to feel bad most of the time, your spouse's best efforts to meet your needs will not make Love Bank deposits. In other words, your depression will make you almost incapable of being in love with him or her. The success of your marriage depends on your ability to be happy—enthusiastic about the way you are living. So if you have been suffering from chronic depression, do yourself and your spouse a huge favor and be treated by a professional therapist.

# 18

## Putting Your Skills to Work

If you've read this far and followed the advice I've given along the way, you've seen how effective negotiation can be. You're getting into the habit of making win-win decisions whenever you have a marital conflict, just like Joyce and I handle our conflicts. You're on your way to a very happy and passion-filled marriage.

But if you've read this book just to see what I have to say, and have not actually started making decisions with mutual enthusiasm, you have probably collected quite a few major conflicts over the years that need your attention as soon as possible. You may be feeling hopeless about resolving them and you may be feeling incredibly incompatible because you have grown so far apart. The love you once felt for each other may now be a distant memory. You may feel that my plan for marital negotiation is too little too late for you.

If that's how you feel, I want to encourage you to give my plan a chance to turn your marriage into everything you hoped it would be. It's been my experience in helping thousands of couples learn to negotiate that such a marriage is not beyond the point of recovery. Coming to enthusiastic agreements about almost everything is possible for any couple.

There are very few couples that begin their marriage with the skill to negotiate effectively, and most of them go through life never learning that skill. As new conflicts enter their lives daily, and pile up because they are unresolved, they eventually come to the conclusion that they are terribly incompatible.

If I could, I would require every high school student to take a class in finding win-win resolutions to marital conflicts, because it would help make their marriages successful. If that class were

### Marriage Builders Resources

In this book, I have offered many ways to find win-win resolutions to marital conflicts. But I would like you to know about other resources you can use to help you think creatively. They can be found on my website, MarriageBuilders.com.

First, there is the Marriage Builders Forum. This is a community of people who come together for marriage support, to answer questions, and to provide advice based on personal experience. It is moderated by those whose marriages have been greatly enriched by following the advice I've provided in this book.

Another source of help is *Marriage Builders Radio*. Joyce and I answer questions that are sent to us by email every weekday on this one-hour radio program that is repeated throughout the day. If we feel that a question has broad relevance and requires a greater depth of understanding, we invite the person with the question to join us on the radio to discuss the issue.

You will find the entire Marriage Builders website to be of help because it includes articles, a Q&A column, and other forms of marital help that are free to those who visit. Millions of couples throughout the world have used this service to help solve the problems they face.

offered, students would all agree that it was among the most valuable skills they learned in school.

But it's a skill that must be learned outside of our educational system. And it's not too late for you to learn it. So if you have not already been following the Policy of Joint Agreement and practicing the Four Guidelines to Successful Negotiation when you face a marital conflict, begin today.

Don't go through life with a loveless, passionless marriage when all it takes to restore your love is to learn how to resolve your conflicts in a way that makes you both happy. Granted, it takes skill to do it, and you may need to practice for a while before you get it right. But once you have that skill, you will be able to have the kind of marriage you have always hoped for, and you will be able to teach your children how they can have a successful marriage, too.

# Marital Negotiation Worksheet

## Step 1: Establish ground rules

**Rule #1:** Try to be pleasant and cheerful throughout your discussion.

**Rule #2:** Put safety first—do not make demands, show disrespect, or become angry when you negotiate.

**Rule #3:** If you reach an impasse where you do not seem to be getting anywhere, or if one of you is starting to make demands, show disrespect, or become angry, stop negotiating and come back to the issue later.

## Step 2: Identify the problem and investigate each other's perspectives

*The Issue:*

*Your Perspective:*

_____

_____

_____

*Your Spouse's Perspective:*

_____

_____

_____

## Step 3: Brainstorm possible solutions

*Possible Solutions:*

_____

_____

_____

_____

_____

_____

_____

_____

_____

_____

_____

_____

**Step 4a:** Choose a solution that meets the conditions of the Policy of Joint Agreement and test that solution for one week

_____

_____

**Step 4b:** Evaluate the effectiveness of your chosen solution and either (a) go back to step 3 to find a new solution if necessary, or (b) continue implementing the current solution

# Emotional Needs Questionnaire

© 1986, 2012 by Willard F. Harley, Jr.

Name _____ Date _____

This questionnaire is designed to help you determine your most important emotional needs and evaluate your spouse's effectiveness in meeting those needs. Answer all the questions as candidly as possible. Do not try to minimize any needs that you feel have been unmet. If your answers require more space, use and attach a separate sheet of paper.

Your spouse should complete a separate Emotional Needs Questionnaire so that you can discover his or her needs and evaluate your effectiveness in meeting those needs.

When you have completed this questionnaire, go through it a second time to be certain your answers accurately reflect your feelings. Do not erase your original answers, but cross them out lightly so that your spouse can see the corrections and discuss them with you.

The final page of this questionnaire asks you to identify and rank five of the ten needs in order of their importance to you. The most important emotional needs are those that give you the most pleasure when met and frustrate you the most when unmet. Resist the temptation to identify as most important only those needs that your spouse is *not* presently meeting. Include *all* your emotional needs in your consideration of those that are most important.

You have the permission of the publisher to photocopy the questionnaire, enlarging to 8½ × 11, for use in your own marriage.

1. **Affection.** The nonsexual expression of care through words, cards, gifts, hugs, kisses, and courtesies; creating an environment that clearly and repeatedly expresses care.

    A. **Need for affection:** Indicate how much you need affection by circling the appropriate number.

| 0 | 1 | 2 | 3 | 4 | 5 | 6 |

I have no need              I have a moderate need           I have a great need
for affection                for affection               for affection

If or when your spouse *is not* affectionate with you, how do you feel? (Circle the appropriate letter.)

    a. Very unhappy        c. Neither happy nor unhappy
    b. Somewhat unhappy    d. Happy not to be shown affection

If or when your spouse is affectionate to you, how do you feel? (Circle the appropriate letter.)

    a. Very happy          c. Neither happy nor unhappy
    b. Somewhat happy     d. Unhappy to be shown affection

    B. **Evaluation of spouse's affection:** Indicate your satisfaction with your spouse's affection toward you by circling the appropriate number.

| −3 | −2 | −1 | 0 | 1 | 2 | 3 |

I am extremely             I am neither satisfied        I am extremely
dissatisfied              nor dissatisfied           satisfied

My spouse gives me all the affection I need.  ☐ Yes  ☐ No

If your answer is no, how often would you like your spouse to be affectionate with you?

    _____ (write number) times each day/week/month (circle one).

I like the way my spouse gives me affection.  ☐ Yes  ☐ No

If your answer is no, explain how your need for affection could be better satisfied in your marriage.

_____

_____

_____

2. **Sexual fulfillment.** A sexual experience that is predictably enjoyable and frequent enough for you.

A. **Need for sexual fulfillment:** Indicate how much you need sexual fulfillment by circling the appropriate number.

| 0 | 1 | 2 | 3 | 4 | 5 | 6 |

I have no need for sexual fulfillment     I have a moderate need for sexual fulfillment     I have a great need for sexual fulfillment

If or when your spouse *is not* willing to engage in sexual relations with you, how do you feel? (Circle the appropriate letter.)

a. Very unhappy     c. Neither happy nor unhappy

b. Somewhat unhappy     d. Happy not to engage in sexual relations

If or when your spouse engages in sexual relations with you, how do you feel? (Circle the appropriate letter.)

a. Very happy     c. Neither happy nor unhappy

b. Somewhat happy     d. Unhappy to engage in sexual relations

B. **Evaluation of sexual relations with your spouse:** Indicate your satisfaction with your spouse's sexual relations with you by circling the appropriate number.

| −3 | −2 | −1 | 0 | 1 | 2 | 3 |

I am extremely dissatisfied     I am neither satisfied nor dissatisfied     I am extremely satisfied

My spouse has sexual relations with me as often as I need. ☐ Yes ☐ No

If your answer is no, how often would you like your spouse to have sex with you?

_____ (write number) times each day/week/month (circle one).

I like the way my spouse has sexual relations with me. ☐ Yes ☐ No

If your answer is no, explain how your need for sexual fulfillment could be better satisfied in your marriage.

_____

_____

_____

3. **Intimate conversation.** Talking about feelings, topics of personal interest/ opinions, and plans.

A. **Need for intimate conversation:** Indicate how much you need intimate conversation by circling the appropriate number.

```
0        1        2        3        4        5        6
```

I have no need                I have a moderate need              I have a great need
for intimate conversation     for intimate conversation          for intimate conversation

If or when your spouse *is not* willing to talk with you, how do you feel? (Circle the appropriate letter.)

a. Very unhappy          c. Neither happy nor unhappy
b. Somewhat unhappy      d. Happy not to talk

If or when your spouse talks to you, how do you feel? (Circle the appropriate letter.)

a. Very happy            c. Neither happy nor unhappy
b. Somewhat happy        d. Unhappy to talk

B. **Evaluation of intimate conversation with your spouse:** Indicate your satisfaction with your spouse's intimate conversation with you by circling the appropriate number.

```
-3       -2       -1        0        1        2        3
```

I am extremely              I am neither satisfied              I am extremely
dissatisfied                nor dissatisfied                    satisfied

My spouse talks to me as often as I need.  ☐ Yes  ☐ No

If your answer is no, how often would you like your spouse to talk to you?

_____ (write number) times each day/week/month (circle one).

_____ (write number) hours each day/week/month (circle one).

I like the way my spouse talks to me.  ☐ Yes  ☐ No

If your answer is no, explain how your need for intimate conversation could be better satisfied in your marriage.

_____

_____

_____

**4. Recreational companionship.** Leisure activities with at least one other person.

**A. Need for recreational companionship:** Indicate how much you need recreational companionship by circling the appropriate number.

| I have no need for recreational companionship | I have a moderate need for recreational companionship | I have a great need for recreational companionship |

If or when your spouse *is not* willing to join you in recreational activities, how do you feel? (Circle the appropriate letter.)

a. Very unhappy     c. Neither happy nor unhappy

b. Somewhat unhappy     d. Happy not to have my spouse join me

If or when your spouse joins you in recreational activities, how do you feel? (Circle the appropriate letter.)

a. Very happy     c. Neither happy nor unhappy

b. Somewhat happy     d. Unhappy to have my spouse join me

**B. Evaluation of recreational companionship with your spouse:** Indicate your satisfaction with your spouse's recreational companionship by circling the appropriate number.

| I am extremely dissatisfied | I am neither satisfied nor dissatisfied | I am extremely satisfied |

My spouse joins me in recreational activities as often as I need.
☐ Yes ☐ No

If your answer is no, how often would you like your spouse to join you in recreational activities?

_____ (write number) times each day/week/month (circle one).

_____ (write number) hours each day/week/month (circle one).

I like the way my spouse joins me in recreational activities. ☐ Yes ☐ No

If your answer is no, explain how your need for recreational companionship could be better satisfied in your marriage.

_____

_____

5. **Honesty and openness.** Truthful and frank expression of positive and negative feelings, events of the past, daily events and schedule, and plans for the future; not leaving a false impression.

A. **Need for honesty and openness:** Indicate how much you need honesty and openness by circling the appropriate number.

| 0 | 1 | 2 | 3 | 4 | 5 | 6 |

I have no need
for honesty and openness

I have a moderate need
for honesty and openness

I have a great need
for honesty and openness

If or when your spouse *is not* open and honest with you, how do you feel? (Circle the appropriate letter.)

a. Very unhappy          c. Neither happy nor unhappy

b. Somewhat unhappy   d. Happy that my spouse isn't honest and open

If or when your spouse is open and honest with you, how do you feel? (Circle the appropriate letter.)

a. Very happy             c. Neither happy nor unhappy

b. Somewhat happy      d. Unhappy that my spouse is honest and open

B. **Evaluation of spouse's honesty and openness:** Indicate your satisfaction with your spouse's honesty and openness by circling the appropriate number.

| −3 | −2 | −1 | 0 | 1 | 2 | 3 |

I am extremely
dissatisfied

I am neither satisfied
nor dissatisfied

I am extremely
satisfied

In which of the following areas of honesty and openness would you like to see improvement from your spouse? (Circle the letters that apply to you.)

a. Sharing positive and negative emotional reactions to significant aspects of life

b. Sharing information regarding his/her personal history

c. Sharing information about his/her daily activities

d. Sharing information about his/her future schedule and plans

If you circled any of the above, explain how your need for honesty and openness could be better satisfied in your marriage.

_____

_____

**6. Physical attractiveness.** Viewing physical traits of the opposite sex that are aesthetically and/or sexually pleasing.

**A. Need for physical attractiveness:** Indicate how much you need physical attractiveness by circling the appropriate number.

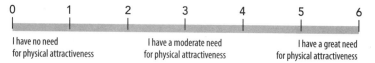

| 0 | 1 | 2 | 3 | 4 | 5 | 6 |

I have no need
for physical attractiveness

I have a moderate need
for physical attractiveness

I have a great need
for physical attractiveness

If or when your spouse *is not* willing to make the most of his or her physical attractiveness, how do you feel? (Circle the appropriate letter.)

a. Very unhappy
b. Somewhat unhappy
c. Neither happy nor unhappy
d. Happy he or she does not make an effort

When your spouse makes the most of his or her physical attractiveness, how do you feel? (Circle the appropriate letter.)

a. Very happy
b. Somewhat happy
c. Neither happy nor unhappy
d. Unhappy to see him or her make an effort

**B. Evaluation of spouse's attractiveness:** Indicate your satisfaction with your spouse's attractiveness by circling the appropriate number.

| -3 | -2 | -1 | 0 | 1 | 2 | 3 |

I am extremely
dissatisfied

I am neither satisfied
nor dissatisfied

I am extremely
satisfied

In which of the following characteristics of attractiveness would you like to see improvement from your spouse? (Circle the letters that apply.)

a. Physical fitness and normal weight
b. Attractive choice of clothes
c. Attractive hairstyle
d. Good physical hygiene
e. Attractive facial makeup
f. Other _____

If you circled any of the above, explain how your need for physical attractiveness could be better satisfied in your marriage.

_____

_____

7. **Financial support.** Provision of the financial resources to house, feed, and clothe your family at a standard of living acceptable to you.

   A. **Need for financial support:** Indicate how much you need financial support by circling the appropriate number.

| 0 | 1 | 2 | 3 | 4 | 5 | 6 |

I have no need
for financial support

I have a moderate need
for financial support

I have a great need
for financial support

   If or when your spouse *is not* willing to support you financially, how do you feel? (Circle the appropriate letter.)

   a. Very unhappy          c. Neither happy nor unhappy

   b. Somewhat unhappy      d. Happy not to be financially supported

   If or when your spouse supports you financially, how do you feel? (Circle the appropriate letter.)

   a. Very happy            c. Neither happy nor unhappy

   b. Somewhat happy        d. Unhappy to be financially supported

   B. **Evaluation of spouse's financial support:** Indicate your satisfaction with your spouse's financial support by circling the appropriate number.

| -3 | -2 | -1 | 0 | 1 | 2 | 3 |

I am extremely
dissatisfied

I am neither satisfied
nor dissatisfied

I am extremely
satisfied

   How much money would you like your spouse to earn to support you?

   _____

   How many hours each week would you like your spouse to work?

   _____

   If your spouse is not earning as much as you would like, is not working the hours you would like, does not budget the way you would like, or does not earn an income the way you would like, explain how your need for financial support could be better satisfied in your marriage.

   _____

   _____

8. **Domestic support.** Management of the household tasks and care of the children—if any are at home—that create a home environment that offers you a refuge from stress.

   A. **Need for domestic support:** Indicate how much you need domestic support by circling the appropriate number.

   | 0 | 1 | 2 | 3 | 4 | 5 | 6 |
   |---|---|---|---|---|---|---|

   I have no need for domestic support        I have a moderate need for domestic support        I have a great need for domestic support

   If your spouse *is not* willing to provide you with domestic support, how do you feel? (Circle the appropriate letter.)

   a. Very unhappy                  c. Neither happy nor unhappy
   b. Somewhat unhappy              d. Happy not to have domestic support

   If or when your spouse provides you with domestic support, how do you feel? (Circle the appropriate letter.)

   a. Very happy                    c. Neither happy nor unhappy
   b. Somewhat happy                d. Unhappy to have domestic support

   B. **Evaluation of spouse's domestic support:** Indicate your satisfaction with your spouse's domestic support by circling the appropriate number.

   | –3 | –2 | –1 | 0 | 1 | 2 | 3 |
   |----|----|----|---|---|---|---|

   I am extremely dissatisfied        I am neither satisfied nor dissatisfied        I am extremely satisfied

   My spouse provides me with all the domestic support I need.
   ☐ Yes  ☐ No

   I like the way my spouse provides domestic support.
   ☐ Yes  ☐ No

   If your answer is no to either of the above questions, explain how your need for domestic support could be better satisfied in your marriage.

   _____

   _____

   _____

   _____

9. **Family commitment.** Provision for the moral and educational development of your children within the family unit.

A. **Need for family commitment:** Indicate how much you need family commitment by circling the appropriate number.

I have no need          I have a moderate need          I have a great need
for family commitment          for family commitment          for family commitment

If or when your spouse *is not* willing to provide family commitment, how do you feel? (Circle the appropriate letter.)

a. Very unhappy          c. Neither happy nor unhappy

b. Somewhat unhappy          d. Happy he or she is not involved

If or when your spouse provides family commitment, how do you feel? (Circle the appropriate letter.)

a. Very happy          c. Neither happy nor unhappy

b. Somewhat happy          d. Unhappy he or she is involved in the family

B. **Evaluation of spouse's family commitment:** Indicate your satisfaction with your spouse's family commitment by circling the appropriate number.

```
-3        -2        -1        0        1        2        3
```

I am extremely          I am neither satisfied          I am extremely
dissatisfied          nor dissatisfied          satisfied

My spouse commits enough time to the family.   ☐ Yes   ☐ No

If your answer is no, how often would you like your spouse to join in family activities?

_____ (write number) times each day/week/month (circle one).

_____ (write number) hours each day/week/month (circle one).

I like the way my spouse spends time with the family.   ☐ Yes   ☐ No

If your answer is no, explain how your need for family commitment could be better satisfied in your marriage.

_____

_____

_____

**10. Admiration.** Being shown respect, value, and appreciation.

A. **Need for admiration:** Indicate how much you need admiration by circling the appropriate number.

| 0 | 1 | 2 | 3 | 4 | 5 | 6 |

I have no need
for admiration

I have a moderate need
for admiration

I have a great need
for admiration

If or when your spouse *does not* admire you, how do you feel? (Circle the appropriate letter.)

a. Very unhappy          c. Neither happy nor unhappy

b. Somewhat unhappy   d. Happy not to be admired

If or when your spouse does admire you, how do you feel? (Circle the appropriate letter.)

a. Very happy            c. Neither happy nor unhappy

b. Somewhat happy     d. Unhappy to be admired

B. **Evaluation of spouse's admiration:** Indicate your satisfaction with your spouse's admiration of you by circling the appropriate number.

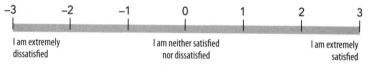

| -3 | -2 | -1 | 0 | 1 | 2 | 3 |

I am extremely
dissatisfied

I am neither satisfied
nor dissatisfied

I am extremely
satisfied

My spouse gives me all the admiration I need.  ☐ Yes  ☐ No

If your answer is no, how often would you like your spouse to admire you?

_____ (write number) times each day/week/month (circle one).

I like the way my spouse admires me.  ☐ Yes  ☐ No

If your answer is no, explain how your need for admiration could be better satisfied in your marriage.

_____

_____

_____

_____

# Ranking Your Emotional Needs

The ten basic emotional needs are listed below. There is also space for you to add other emotional needs that you feel are essential to your marital happiness.

In the space provided before each need, write a number from 1 to 5 that ranks the need's importance to your happiness. Write a 1 before the most important need, a 2 before the next most important, and so on until you have ranked your five most important needs.

To help you rank these needs, imagine that you will have only one need met in your marriage. Which would make you the happiest, knowing that all the others would go unmet? That need should be 1. If only two needs will be met, what would your second selection be? Which five needs, when met, would make you the happiest?

_____ Affection

_____ Sexual fulfillment

_____ Intimate conversation

_____ Recreational companionship

_____ Honesty and openness

_____ Physical attractiveness of spouse

_____ Financial support

_____ Domestic support

_____ Family commitment

_____ Admiration

_____ _____

_____ _____

# Appendix C

# Love Busters Questionnaire

© 1992, 2013 by Willard F. Harley, Jr.

Name _____ Date _____

This questionnaire is designed to help identify your spouse's Love Busters. Your spouse engages in a Love Buster whenever one of his or her habits causes you to be unhappy. By causing your unhappiness, your spouse withdraws love units from your Love Bank, and that, in turn, threatens your romantic love for him or her.

There are six categories of Love Busters. Each category has its own set of questions in this questionnaire. Answer all the questions as candidly as possible. Do not try to minimize your unhappiness with your spouse's behavior. If your answers require more space, use and attach a separate sheet of paper.

When you have completed this questionnaire, go through it a second time to be certain your answers accurately reflect your feelings. Do not erase your original answers, but cross them out lightly so that your spouse can see the corrections and discuss them with you.

When you have completed this questionnaire, rank the six Love Busters in order of their importance to you. When you have finished ranking the Love Busters, you may find that your answers to the questions regarding each Love Buster are inconsistent with your final ranking. This inconsistency is common. It often reflects a less-than-perfect understanding of your feelings. If you notice inconsistencies, discuss them with your spouse to help clarify your feelings.

You have the permission of the publisher to photocopy the questionnaire, enlarging to 8½ × 11, for use in your own marriage.

1. **Selfish Demands:** Attempts by your spouse to force you to do something for him or her, usually with implied threat of punishment if you refuse.

   A. **Selfish Demands as a Cause of Unhappiness:** Indicate how much unhappiness you tend to experience when your spouse makes selfish demands of you.

   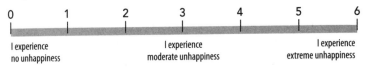

   | 0 | 1 | 2 | 3 | 4 | 5 | 6 |

   I experience            I experience            I experience
   no unhappiness     moderate unhappiness     extreme unhappiness

   B. **Frequency of Spouse's Selfish Demands:** Indicate how often your spouse makes selfish demands of you.

   _____ selfish demands each day/week/month/year.
   (write number)                                 (circle one)

   C. **Form(s) Selfish Demands Take:** When your spouse makes selfish demands of you, what does he or she typically do?

   _____

   _____

   D. **Form of Selfish Demands That Causes the Greatest Unhappiness:** Which of the above forms of selfish demands causes you the greatest unhappiness?

   _____

   _____

   E. **Onset of Selfish Demands:** When did your spouse first make selfish demands of you?

   _____

   _____

   F. **Development of Selfish Demands:** Have your spouse's selfish demands increased or decreased in intensity and/or frequency since they first began? How do recent selfish demands compare to those of the past?

   _____

   _____

2. **Disrespectful Judgments:** Attempts by your spouse to change your attitudes, beliefs, and behavior by trying to force you into his or her way of thinking.

   A. **Disrespectful Judgments as a Cause of Unhappiness:** Indicate how much unhappiness you tend to experience when your spouse engages in disrespectful judgments toward you.

   | 0 | 1 | 2 | 3 | 4 | 5 | 6 |
   |---|---|---|---|---|---|---|

   I experience no unhappiness   I experience moderate unhappiness   I experience extreme unhappiness

   B. **Frequency of Spouse's Disrespectful Judgments:** Indicate how often your spouse tends to engage in disrespectful judgments toward you.

   _____ disrespectful judgments each day/week/month/year.

   (write number)                                            (circle one)

   C. **Form(s) Disrespectful Judgments Take:** When your spouse engages in disrespectful judgments toward you, what does he or she typically do?

   _____

   _____

   D. **Form of Disrespectful Judgments That Causes the Greatest Unhappiness:** Which of the above forms of disrespectful judgments causes you the greatest unhappiness?

   _____

   _____

   E. **Onset of Disrespectful Judgments:** When did your spouse first engage in disrespectful judgments toward you?

   _____

   _____

   F. **Development of Disrespectful Judgments:** Have your spouse's disrespectful judgments increased or decreased in intensity and/or frequency since they first began? How do recent disrespectful judgments compare to those of the past?

   _____

**3. Angry Outbursts:** Deliberate attempts by your spouse to hurt you because of anger toward you. They are usually in the form of verbal or physical attacks.

**A. Angry Outbursts as a Cause of Unhappiness:** Indicate how much unhappiness you tend to experience when your spouse attacks you with an angry outburst.

| 0 | 1 | 2 | 3 | 4 | 5 | 6 |

I experience
no unhappiness

I experience
moderate unhappiness

I experience
extreme unhappiness

**B. Frequency of Spouse's Angry Outbursts:** Indicate how often your spouse tends to engage in angry outbursts toward you.

_____ angry outbursts each day/week/month/ year.

(write number)                                                          (circle one)

**C. Form(s) Angry Outbursts Take:** When your spouse engages in angry outbursts toward you, what does he or she typically do?

_____

_____

**D. Form of Angry Outbursts That Causes the Greatest Unhappiness:** Which of the above forms of angry outbursts causes you the greatest unhappiness?

_____

_____

**E. Onset of Angry Outbursts:** When did your spouse first engage in angry outbursts toward you?

_____

_____

**F. Development of Angry Outbursts:** Have your spouse's angry outbursts increased or decreased in intensity and/or frequency since they first began? How do recent angry outbursts compare to those of the past?

_____

_____

178

4. **Dishonesty:** Failure of your spouse to reveal his or her thoughts, feelings, habits, likes, dislikes, personal history, daily activities, and plans for the future. Dishonesty is not only providing false information about any of the above topics, but it is also leaving you with what he or she knows is a false impression.

A. **Dishonesty as a Cause of Unhappiness:** Indicate how much unhappiness you tend to experience when your spouse is dishonest with you.

B. **Frequency of Spouse's Dishonesty:** Indicate how often your spouse tends to be dishonest with you.

_____ instances of dishonesty each day/week/month/year.

(write number)                                                                                          (circle one)

C. **Form(s) Dishonesty Takes:** When your spouse is dishonest with you, what does he or she typically do?

_____

_____

D. **Form of Dishonesty That Causes the Greatest Unhappiness:** Which of the above forms of dishonesty causes you the greatest unhappiness?

_____

_____

E. **Onset of Dishonesty:** When was your spouse first dishonest with you?

_____

_____

F. **Development of Dishonesty:** Has your spouse's dishonesty increased or decreased in intensity and/or frequency since it first began? How do recent instances of dishonesty compare to those of the past?

_____

_____

5. **Annoying Habits:** Behavior repeated by your spouse without much thought that bothers you. These habits include personal mannerisms such as the way your spouse eats, cleans up after him- or herself, and talks.

   A. **Annoying Habits as a Cause of Unhappiness:** Indicate how much unhappiness you tend to experience when your spouse engages in annoying habits.

   0     1     2     3     4     5     6

   I experience no unhappiness     I experience moderate unhappiness     I experience extreme unhappiness

   B. **Frequency of Spouse's Annoying Habits:** Indicate how often your spouse tends to engage in annoying habits.

   _____ occurrences of annoying habits each day/week/month/year.
   (write number)     (circle one)

   C. **Form(s) Annoying Habits Takes:** When your spouse engages in annoying habits toward you, what does he or she typically do?

   _____

   _____

   D. **Form of Annoying Habits That Causes the Greatest Unhappiness:** Which of the above forms of annoying habits causes you the greatest unhappiness?

   _____

   _____

   E. **Onset of Annoying Habits:** When did your spouse first engage in annoying habits?

   _____

   _____

   F. **Development of Annoying Habits:** Have your spouse's annoying habits increased or decreased in intensity and/or frequency since they first began? How do those recent annoying habits compare to those of the past?

   _____

   _____

6. **Independent Behavior:** Behavior conceived and executed by your spouse without consideration of your feelings. These behaviors are usually scheduled and require thought to complete, such as attending sporting events or engaging in a personal exercise program.

   A. **Independent Behavior as a Cause of Unhappiness:** Indicate how much unhappiness you tend to experience when your spouse engages in independent behavior.

   | 0 | 1 | 2 | 3 | 4 | 5 | 6 |

   I experience        I experience              I experience
   no unhappiness      moderate unhappiness      extreme unhappiness

   B. **Frequency of Spouse's Independent Behavior:** Indicate how often your spouse tends to engage in independent behavior.

   _____ occurrences of independent behavior each day/week/month/year.
   (write number)                                                    (circle one)

   C. **Form(s) Independent Behavior Takes:** When your spouse engages in independent behavior toward you, what does he or she typically do?

   _____

   _____

   D. **Form of Independent Behavior That Causes the Greatest Unhappiness:** Which of the above forms of independent behavior causes you the greatest unhappiness?

   _____

   _____

   E. **Onset of Independent Behavior:** When did your spouse first engage in independent behavior?

   _____

   _____

   F. **Development of Independent Behavior:** Has your spouse's independent behavior increased or decreased in intensity and/or frequency since it first began? How does recent independent behavior compare to that of the past?

   _____

# Ranking Love Busters

The six basic categories of Love Busters are listed below. There is also space for you to add other categories of Love Busters that you feel contribute to your marital unhappiness. In the space provided in front of each Love Buster, write a number from 1 to 6 that ranks its relative contribution to your unhappiness. Write a 1 before the Love Buster that causes you the greatest unhappiness, a 2 before the one causing the next greatest unhappiness, and so on, until you have ranked all six.

_____ Selfish Demands

_____ Disrespectful Judgments

_____ Angry Outbursts

_____ Annoying Habits

_____ Independent Behavior

_____ Dishonesty

_____  _____

_____  _____

Dr. Willard F. Harley, Jr., is a nationally acclaimed clinical psychologist, marriage counselor, and bestselling author. His popular website, MarriageBuilders.com, offers practical solutions to almost any marital problem. He and Joyce, his wife of over fifty years, host a daily radio call-in show, *Marriage Builders Radio*. They live in White Bear Lake, Minnesota.

# The best book on marriage is now
## *better than ever!*

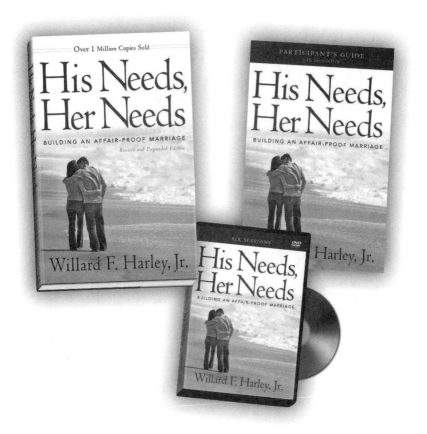

For over twenty-five years, *His Needs, Her Needs* has been transforming marriages all over the world. Now this life-changing book is the basis for an interactive six-week DVD study designed for use in couples' small groups or retreats, in premarital counseling sessions, or by individual couples.

# The best marriage workbook
## *just got better!*

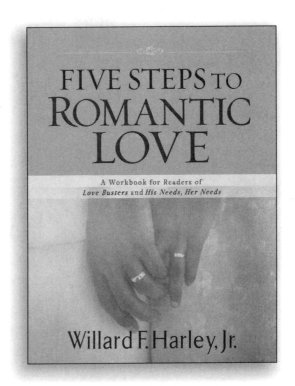

*Five Steps to Romantic Love* will help you and your spouse to know and meet each other's needs and overcome the habits that destroy your love. This workbook is a supplement to Dr. Harley's *Love Busters* and *His Needs, Her Needs*—books that have helped countless couples fall in love again and enjoy intimate, passionate marriages.

# ACHIEVE A DEEPER RELATIONSHIP WITH GOD AND WITH EACH OTHER

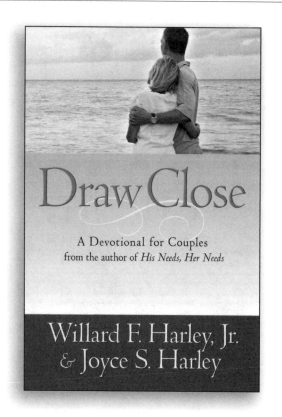

In our rushed and busy world, time is at a premium—and quality time spent with God and with your spouse is often a casualty. Nothing can bring you closer to both God and each other quite like sharing a daily devotional time.

**Я Revell**
a division of Baker Publishing Group
www.RevellBooks.com

# Enjoy a romantic, passionate,
## *lifelong marriage!*

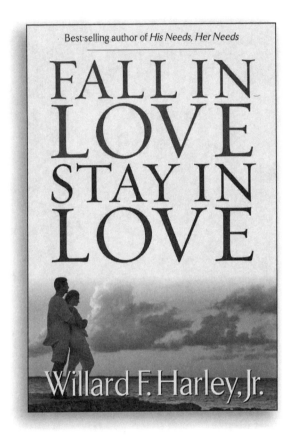

Dr. Harley has spent more than thirty years helping couples create, re-create, and sustain romantic love. In this foundational book, he provides you with all the tools you'll need to fall in love and stay in love with your spouse.

# Are you *losing the love* you once felt for each other?

From Dr. Harley, the author of *His Needs, Her Needs*, comes a book that will help you identify the six Love Busters that pull marriages apart, and will show you and your spouse how to avoid them. The strength of your marriage depends on the passion you share for each other. So stop destroying the feeling of love and discover, instead, how to build your love with care and with time.

# MARRIAGE BUILDERS®
## *Building Marriages To Last A Lifetime*

At MarriageBuilders.com, Dr. Harley introduces you to the best ways to overcome marital conflicts and the quickest ways to restore love.

Read Dr. Harley's articles, follow the Q&A columns, interact with other couples on the Forum, and listen to Dr. Harley and his wife Joyce answer your questions on Marriage Builders® Radio. Learn to become an expert in making your marriage the best it can be.

*Let Marriage Builders® help you build a marriage to last a lifetime!*
www.marriagebuilders.com